Praise for *Life and Soul*

LIFE AND SOUL

LIFE AND SOUL

How to Live a Long and Healthy Life

WILLIAM ROACHE

HAY HOUSE

Carlsbad, California • New York City
London • Sydney • New Delhi

Published in the United Kingdom by:
Hay House UK Ltd, The Sixth Floor, Watson House
54 Baker Street, London W1U 7BU
Tel: +44 (0)20 3927 7290; Fax: +44 (0)20 3927 7291
www.hayhouse.co.uk

Published in the United States of America by:
Hay House Inc., PO Box 5100, Carlsbad, CA 92018-5100
Tel: (1) 760 431 7695 or (800) 654 5126; Fax: (1) 760 431 6948 or (800) 650 5115
www.hayhouse.com

Published in Australia by:
Hay House Australia Ltd, 18/36 Ralph St, Alexandria NSW 2015
Tel: (61) 2 9669 4299; Fax: (61) 2 9669 4144
www.hayhouse.com.au

Published in India by:
Hay House Publishers India, Muskaan Complex, Plot No.3, B-2,
Vasant Kunj, New Delhi 110 070
Tel: (91) 11 4176 1620; Fax: (91) 11 4176 1630
www.hayhouse.co.in

A catalogue record for this book is available from the British Library.

Hardback ISBN: 978-1-78180-977-8
E-book ISBN: 978-1-78817-036-9
Audiobook ISBN: 978-1-78817-218-9
Tradepaper ISBN: 978-1-78817-353-7

Printed and bound in Great Britain by
TJ International Ltd, Padstow, Cornwall

MIX
Paper from
responsible sources
FSC® C013056

In this book I am writing from my own experience and my own knowing. If it resonates with you and helps your understanding, that is good. If it doesn't resonate with you or you disagree with anything, that is good too. You must always go with your own knowing. I am not stating how things are, just how I see and understand them. I am wary of beliefs as they can be fickle and changeable, but I am always looking for the truth, which never changes.

As you read this, may you receive love, understanding and healing.

To my children

CONTENTS

PREFACE

This book wasn't our father's idea. It was Will's, and it came to him because so many people have asked us, 'What does your father do? What's his secret? He looks young for his age and he is so young at heart.'

We ourselves have always talked about how amazing he is and how different his outlook is, and so we decided to raise the idea of a self-help book with him.

His first response was, 'Really? But I don't do much, you know. I don't have a special diet or do lots of exercise or anything. I just live in a way that suits me. It's just about being relaxed...'

As we talked more, we began to see just how much this relaxed attitude has helped him. There's no ego, no stress or agitation in his life, and because of this there's no inner turmoil, and that definitely contributes to his wellbeing. Stress eats away at people, and this hasn't happened to our father; and it not only benefits him, but also everyone who comes into contact with him. When we go to stay, it's like going to an amazing resort. Home is a sanctuary, and we just can't feel stressed when we're there. In any case, he'll tell us, 'Rest, just rest. Relax.'

He's a humble person. He'd never presume to know better than anyone else, let alone advise them. He won't impose his views on anyone, or try to change them; he'll just go forwards with his own understanding of life. Over a few conversations, though, we all began to see how simply explaining what works for him could help other people too, and he was happy to do that. Our father is probably one of the kindest and most modest people on the planet.

We're an incredibly close family. We've always said our father is our best friend as well, and has been our whole lives. We're so lucky, having him as our beacon of safety and comfort. He's always listened to us and supported us with unconditional love. Any worry we have, any query, any question, it's always, 'Got to ask Daddy.' And we know then that everything will be all right.

When we've had tough times, like when our mother died, we've made sure not to distance ourselves or hide away. If you're going through something and go into your own turmoil, you're not there for others. You have to stay open, to communicate, and we've always been able to do that. When we lost our mother, we talked about how we felt all the time; keeping that dialogue open was so important. And we lifted one another up, as well as allowed one another space when we needed it.

Through going through bereavement and through issues with the media, we've stuck to one another so closely, and to our brother and sister, Linus and Vanya, too. This closeness has supported us through difficult experiences, although we've all had to experience certain things in our own way and in our own time.

We had to find our own way to heal after our mother died. Looking back, we both rushed into other things too soon. I, Will, was in the middle of filming *Four Seasons*, a TV mini-series, and about four days after the funeral I had to go back and do the second episode. I totally get people throwing themselves into work for distraction, but looking back, I was in a weird haze; I was in shock. Had that job been a month or two later, I probably would have welcomed it. And I, Verity, threw myself into an intensive interior design course. I'd had a few months at home after our mother's funeral, but it was still too soon, too harsh for me at the time. I went from being very self-protective, being with our father in Wilmslow, to thrusting myself back into London and into education, because that's what I thought I should do. And it wasn't right for me. I think I was a bit too forceful with myself. But together, we got through it, and it brought us even closer. It made us stronger as a family.

We know that whatever's happening, you've got to make peace with the situation you're in and do what you can do – which is to make one another feel better, to comfort one another, to try to stay relaxed and to laugh whenever you can.

We laugh a lot. We always have so much fun together, whatever we're doing. Our father will say, 'I'm going to see this. Do you want to come along? I don't know what it's going to be like,' and no matter what it's like, we know we'll have a great time.

Partly this is because he's so funny. He's a wonderful giggler, and sometimes he just can't stop. He'll be crying with laughter at the comedies we watch, and especially at his own jokes. If he tells a joke, he'll be laughing so much, he'll often be unable to get to the punchline. He'll say, 'I find my jokes funny. Why would I tell them if I didn't find them funny?'

I suppose we've always felt people haven't had a chance to see this side of him enough. Some people have seen it, though. When I, Verity, was at school, he was visiting one day and noticed that the mannequin displaying our school uniform was a little off-kilter. So he tried to help by adjusting the arm and ended up with the whole mannequin falling to bits and going everywhere. Seeing him trying to help and then ending up in a Frank Spencer situation made us all laugh so much.

He also loved the big banisters in the school hall, which were quite grand and swooping. He said they reminded him of the ones in his old house, and one day, as there seemed to be no teachers around, he couldn't resist sliding down them like a schoolboy. We were giggling so hard and loving the feeling of freedom, seeing a parent breaking the rules. I was only about 10 years old at the time, but Daddy would have been around 60, and he was behaving in the most fun and free way – more than I was! He has helped me to have fun with things and not to be too serious all the time. He always seems to have that perfect balance between responsibility and irreverence. He'd never laugh inappropriately, but he knows where there is space for fun. It's about making the most of the good times, whatever's going on.

In fact, our father is incredible. His outlook is just amazing – and *we're* saying this because *he* won't! He just thinks really positively all the time. Negatives don't come into it; he doesn't talk about his age, for one thing, and never says, 'In my day…' He's forward-thinking and lives in the moment. And he lives that way so naturally.

Just as he has always helped us, we hope this book helps you, too.

Verity and Will Roache
July 2017

ACKNOWLEDGEMENTS

I would like to thank Liz Dean for her inspirational help in writing this book, the Hay House team for all their good work and encouragement, John Hayes and Champions for their help and support, and James Wood and Ann Rogers for their love and advice.

Special thanks to all my family, especially Will and Verity, for their love, and for inspiring me to write this book.

INTRODUCTION

Ten years ago, in 2007, I wrote an autobiography, *Soul on the Street*. That was the first time I had talked openly about my life – not just as Ken Barlow, but as William Roache. The book was well received, and I still get letters from readers across the globe sharing their spiritual experiences. This book is the next episode, and much more: it's a self-help guide to physical and spiritual wellbeing. My aim here is to share with you some of the truths and practices I have learned along the way that continue to benefit me, in the hope that some will resonate with you and be helpful to you, too.

The last decade has been bitter-sweet for me. There have been joyful times and intense personal challenges, times when I felt incredibly spiritually uplifted and days when meditation became my sole refuge. Some of what follows has been painful to relate. Yet the challenges have given me an even deeper understanding of my place and purpose in the world, and the good health, peace and energy I now enjoy come from this knowledge.

So this book is, overall, an invitation to wellbeing, however you want to experience it. You may want relief from stress and overthinking, guidance on eating well or advice on how to recover your vitality in some way. The information in these pages comes from my experience and inner guidance. I'm no doctor, unlike my father, but what you'd call a 'seeker of truth'. Truth is found through the heart and feelings rather than the head and reasoning. Anxiety and stress come from the head, whereas the heart holds the truth of who we are and can guide us to live in a more joyful, peaceful and positive way.

I've found it has worked for me. At 85 (86, I hope, by the time you read this!), I feel good. I've lived long enough to have experienced many things and learned many lessons, which I will share with you here. But I'm getting ahead of myself. First let me tell you a little about my background.

I come from a long line of doctors, but have among my ancestors some unconventional people who sought the truth in their own way. My paternal grandfather, William, was a doctor, surgeon, theosophist, spiritualist and hypnotist, inhabiting the worlds of both science and spirit. My maternal great-grandfather, James Waddicor, was a phrenologist and what was then known as a 'medical electrician', administering mild electric shocks to the day trippers on Blackpool's thriving seafront to treat a range of ailments. 'Electrotherapy' was popular during the Victorian era and probably cost much less than calling the doctor. It's not something I'll be recommending in this book, though!

My grandfather William was an incredibly compassionate and generous man. I never knew him, but I am still inspired by his memory. He was instrumental in facilitating the establishment of one of the early Steiner schools, Michael House, by donating half of the garden of our family home, Rutland House in Ilkeston, Derbyshire, to the Rudolph Steiner Society. We had a large house and garden, as the house was also the doctor's surgery. The new Steiner school opened in 1934, seven years after my grandfather died, but his gift of land was just the beginning. The school eventually moved to larger premises up the road, near Shipley. During those early years, though, I had the benefit of growing up next door to it and hearing the children's laughter over the garden hedge.

The Steiner philosophy on education is still pioneering: it advocates a holistic approach, emphasizing that learning should be joyful, relaxed and non-denominational, and that the interests of the child should be encouraged. I soon discovered this when I attended Michael House myself – it was two-and-a-half years of creativity and fun that I know helped shape the quest for spiritual truth that was to come.

When I later went to the Methodist Rydal School in Colwyn Bay, I couldn't help but challenge the theology master – I was probably the most irritating pupil he had, always wanting answers (rather than 'God works in mysterious ways') and refusing to acknowledge accepted beliefs. I've always needed to know why we're here and what happens after death, and I've always felt there's so much more to life than our normal perception of it.

My pioneering grandfather was also interested in all things otherworldly, and so too were his sisters, Mabel and Mickey. They were Spiritualists at the height of the Spiritualist movement in the early 1900s.

My mother and father were never curious about the unseen worlds beyond ours, so the quest for answers skipped a generation and landed firmly with me. Over the years, I've explored many paths: druidry, Hinduism and Buddhism, theosophy and astrology, as well as the family favourite, Spiritualism. I don't identify with any religion or belief system now, I just follow my own path of love, truth and gratitude to Source, the creator of All That Is, and aim to work in harmony with that Source towards the great goal of world peace.

I refer to Source quite a lot in this book. You might prefer 'the divine father', 'the absolute deity', 'the supreme being', 'the Almighty', 'God', 'the God of gods' – just use whichever name is most meaningful to you. None of these words can fully describe the true majesty of this supreme being, but we do need a name!

I also use the word 'universe' in this book. This is the same as Source. 'Universe' refers to our universe. It is more focused, and 'Source' includes everything: all universes, All That Is. It is the one energy from which everything is created, and that is the energy of love.

Many experiences have shown me the existence of Source and the nature of the soul. After the death of the physical body, the soul returns to heaven, which is our eternal home. Our loved ones continue to be with us there, and other souls and entities are with us during our lifetimes to guide and protect us. When we come to Earth, we program ourselves to attract certain situations, and these give us the experiences that we need for soul expression. So we should aim to embrace them and deal with them with love and courage, as they are there to help us on our eternal journey.

In *Soul on the Street*, I wrote about my special relationship with Peggy Kennard, a gifted medium who passed on many loving messages from my beloved daughter Edwina, who died at 18 months old. Through Peggy, Edwina let me know that she was now a nurse, helping children who had passed over and were asking for their mothers.

While Peggy's messages brought me great comfort at the time, I've had no urge to receive further messages through mediums. Although these can be of interest sometimes, I don't need them now. I am more interested in finding out about life and the great truths, and I do this by going inwards. My 'going inwards' means going into my heart; the key to the kingdom of Source, or God, is through the heart rather than the head. And when you feel connected to Source, to the energy of love, the quality of your life is enhanced beyond belief.

I now read less and meditate more. Other than Ken's scripts for work, I take only the occasional dive into a spiritual book; if I need to know something, I just go into my heart and into my essence, my true being. I send Edwina love and I send love to my late wife Sara, and I know that this is received, because love is the great connector. Sara died suddenly in 2009, at the age of 58, but she's with me in spirit; love never dies.

Living alone without her, however, came as a huge shock. We are all changed by our experiences, but there is always something to learn, no matter how crushing these things feel at the time. I take this learning forwards and am optimistic, always, about the future. The universe is always moving us towards what is best for us. I'm thankful for everything, and I enjoy life.

The journey to wellbeing and contentment always begins with ourselves. That's not to say we must be selfish, far from it; it's about going within to find the truth and the knowing that is inside us – the happiness, the health, the peace, energy and positivity.

My view is this: *health and happiness begin with knowing ourselves*. It's tempting to rush around trying to fix ourselves, but it all starts with how we think and who we think we are. No diet or random system of belief will work on its own. We might try a new regime of healthy eating and exercise, but soon revert to old habits. But when we begin to know ourselves from the heart, we see the world differently and become more relaxed and ready to take the actions that make life more abundant, creative and enjoyable. We take responsibility for ourselves, and by looking after ourselves, we are able to look after others.

I've put this book together in a way that I hope takes you on a journey to health, happiness and understanding. In the first chapter, *Living from the Heart*, are the meditation techniques that have kept me going during the darkest times, such as dealing with the loss of Sara and my screen wife, Annie Kirkbride, whom I talk about in Chapter 2. The third chapter, *Love, Forgiveness and Wellbeing*, invites you to look at the power of forgiveness and the importance of living in a balanced way. For me, it's all about moderation, common sense and enjoyment. Then in Chapter 4 we go to court, and I reveal the challenges and gifts of my year out from the Street. In Chapter 5, *Lifelong Wellbeing*, I talk about my diet and exercise – how I eat, how I overcame Type II diabetes and how I renew my body's cells. The next chapter, *Inspirational People*, takes us around the world to see how other healthy older people are thriving, and examines what they have in common. When researching this chapter, I found so many inspiring people who, through their own natural knowing, are way ahead of some of the scientific research into longevity. And the final chapter, *Living in the Present*, takes a look at how enjoying the present helps the future look after itself.

No matter what age you are or what your life has been about up to this point, this book may have something for you. You might read it from cover to cover or prefer to dip in and out, just taking what you need. The fact that you're reading it at all means you're ready to think about some change in your life. There's no need to do anything big or drastic. As I explain further on, the things we think of as small aren't small at all. Small changes are big things. You can make very simple adjustments to your daily routine and see a big difference in how you feel. And once you begin, you'll find that positive life experiences open up for you. You'll benefit from more energy and less stress, and start to care for your body. You'll discover that being loving, kind and compassionate, especially to yourself, is an expression of who you really are. And you'll start to be grateful for all that you have.

I have experienced this in my own life. Now I am sharing what I have discovered with you in the hope that it may resonate with you and help you.

With love,
Bill

Chapter 1

LIVING FROM THE HEART

My throat was tight and my heart was racing. I knew what was about to happen, because it had happened the day before. I knew when I opened my mouth the line I was supposed to say, Ken's line, wouldn't be there. I didn't have the words; all I had was this numb blank panic. I suddenly couldn't remember one line of the script.

It wasn't as if I was new to the set – I'd been a part of *Coronation Street* for at least 20 years at that point. Yet out of the blue I was just drying up. It was terrifying, and I couldn't understand why it was happening.

I tried working even harder at learning my lines before arriving at the studios. But when I came to deliver them, I would feel that panic rising and my mind going blank. On one occasion, I even had to say that I wasn't feeling well and go back to my dressing room. Soon it got so bad that I was dreading going into work and breaking out in a sweat at the thought of having to do scenes. I knew this happened to a lot of actors; Laurence Olivier, whom I had met right at the start of my career, went through a bad phase of it, and quite a few actors had had to give up theatre work and turn to films for that reason. But that wasn't much comfort when I was in full make-up under the lights.

Fortunately, by this time I'd been meditating for about 10 years. So I took this problem into the silence with me. (That's one of my terms for meditating, as I feel it as a silence.) Immediately I realized that I had let fear in. This is something that we do too easily and too often. We should be on our guard against it, otherwise it becomes a habit. This had been the case with me, and it should have been glaringly obvious, but it had happened gradually, and I only got the full realization when I took the problem with me into meditation.

I knew that fear disappeared when you faced it, and that fear could not exist where there was love, so I really started to focus on my love of acting – the love of the words, the enjoyment of acting, the pleasure of going into work and the love of *Coronation Street*. Quite quickly, the fear dissolved and everything returned to normal.

14

Meditation Opens the Door to the Heart

I've been an actor for over 60 years now, and I've been meditating for around 50 of those years. It's so much a part of me now, I barely think of it as 'meditation', just a really positive way of being, and it's helped me be peaceful and happy and look to the future.

When I first began meditating, though, it wasn't at all what I expected. I thought it would help me to relax. Yet when I first tried it, back in the 1960s, I found a lot of anger in there. I had found a quiet place, sat down, got the posture right, started thinking of a peaceful seashore and waves coming in and out, and allowed my breath to follow that rhythm. But my mind was racing, my emotions were racing, my body was fidgeting and I thought, *What's this? What's going on?*

I couldn't believe it. I thought I'd feel instantly calm and that my first experience of meditation would be pleasant and dreamy. I'd no idea I'd feel stressed and angry.

What was happening was that I was experiencing myself as I truly was, not how I thought I was. Looking back, this shouldn't have been surprising. That state of restlessness and irritation is one that many of us live in, and it was how I was living at that time: feeling depleted and empty, and knowing something was lacking within me.

I recognize now that when I first started meditating, my anger was actually a kind of fear of letting go. At the time, I was successful at my job, I was earning regular money and most people would have thought, *What's he got to worry about?* But I was very unhappy. The way I was living – drinking, smoking, and so on – just didn't feel right. I knew I wasn't a bad person; I just wasn't living in a way that suited me. I felt wrong. This was my conscience talking to me. Our conscience is our eternal self, which guides us, gives us ideas and looks after us – so always listen to your conscience; it knows when you need help!

Luckily, I found help. Through a friend, I found a homoeopathic doctor based in Dulwich, south London, called Dr Thomas Maugham. He also taught meditation, although that was only a small part of the journey this great teacher was about to take me on. Exhausted mentally, physically and spiritually, I was seeking something, and he knew what I needed. At his weekly meetings I slowly began to understand some great truths. I started to let go and open up.

I know I found Dr Maugham because I was ready. They say that the teacher comes when the pupil is ready, and it's an old adage, but it's true. A teacher will present themselves to us when we've done the work we need to do; it's a bit like going from kindergarten to primary school and university, and so on. Whatever we need will come in on our level, when we're in a position to learn. You may be reading this book because you're ready to learn, and I hope it guides you, in some small way, on your journey to better health, peace, truth and love.

Over my years of meditation practice, I began to understand that my mind and heart needed to work together in harmony. We tend to think the mind is the great power, that everything comes from the mind. But if the mind isn't connected to the heart, it strays all over the place, and unfortunate and stressful events can come about. The mind latches on to too much detail, forgetting the calmer, bigger picture of the heart.

Gradually I learned to take no notice of the passing irritations of the mind and to concentrate on the bigger picture and understand my eternal self. When this happens, we gain perspective and see the nature of our problems. And those problems become minor; we realize they aren't the major things we thought they were. We may worry about money and relationships, and of course we can't ignore them – they must be dealt with. But if we're immersed in them and totally attached to them or worried about them, we can't make any real judgements about them – we can't deal with them properly.

It's rather like battling through the jungle with a machete. Somehow or other we get through, but life is much easier if we can find ourselves within the truer picture, the picture of who and what we are, which is always loving and calm and truthful. You might describe this feeling of the bigger picture as 'being centred'. But being centred can imply something small, whereas centredness is expansive; it embraces everything. And we need this centredness, because life throws challenges at us all the time. Life is about experiences and, while we don't want to miss out on experiences, we do want to be able deal with them from the larger eternal perspective. Meditation will help us to have this perspective.

Now, it's not essential to meditate – some people can reach that state of peace and oneness without it. But for many people, meditation is the most helpful method. And it has helped me tremendously – not only to survive some really tough times in my personal and professional life, but also to grow as a human being, live well, be relaxed and have the energy I need. It helps me to balance the demands of being in the public eye and be who I am at heart. It also helps my awareness and understanding to grow.

Just one of the key benefits of meditation is a lowering of stress levels. Meditation opens a door for you to go into your heart, which is always a place of loving calm. Stress just isn't there. Stress is in the mind; peace is in the heart.

Stress has such a huge impact on health, and we don't pay it enough attention. If we have lots of stress, we just hope that it goes away, but we wouldn't take that approach with a broken bone or any other kind of physical ailment that could damage our body. And stress harms us. It raises our blood pressure, which can be damaging to the heart; it also depletes our immune system, which is why we get a cold when we're due to do something important – anything from attending a meeting to getting on a plane. And being stressed doesn't help if we're trying to eat well, because it can make us crave those twin comforts of fat and sugar. For many of us, stress triggers comfort eating, or turns us off food altogether. It certainly interferes with our appetite and digestive processes.

We can see this in animals as well as people, such as when a pet won't eat because they are stressed or unhappy. Our little Jack Russell, Poppy, got dangerously ill when her companion, Harry, died. Now they hadn't exactly been best friends when he was alive – they seemed to irritate each other and were more rivals than anything – but Poppy became really stressed when she was alone. She got so ill that the vet told us she wouldn't survive.

My daughter Verity refused to accept this and decided to take charge of her immediately. She took her home to London, where she could nurse her every day, and started by giving her Reiki healing. There was an immediate recovery, and Verity followed up on this by making some changes to Poppy's diet – giving her blended fresh, raw vegetables of varying colours with milk thistle, a remedy to reduce inflammation and help digestion. It was really important for Poppy to have a 'living' diet – natural, organic, chemical-free foods full of life-force (unlike some processed dog foods, which can sit on supermarket shelves for two years and are full of preservatives). Within a few weeks, the vet was astounded – Poppy's blood sugar results were normal. He gave Verity print-outs of the results before and after, which I still have pinned to the fridge in the family kitchen. Now, one year on, Poppy, at 14 – that's 78 in human years – has bags of energy. She's not stressed; she's happy and healthy again, and when she meets people they ask if she's a puppy.

Because stress can creep up on us, we can become used to feeling agitated and anxious. And we live in very busy, stressful times. The brain is too busy, the mind too full of complexity and detail. We need to move into the heart, for that is where the true self is, and the heart sees the bigger picture. Meditation guides us into our heart. It's like opening a door that takes us to our true self – the self that has health and energy, the self that is calm, creative, compassionate, loving and strong.

Meditation helps us relax, too, and when we're relaxed, everything in life is better. If we meditate regularly, we'll find that we become more receptive to things, we're more intuitive, and truth comes more readily to us, because we see it everywhere. And what happens is that the mind and heart begin to work together in a calm way. We feel more at peace, and from that peaceful place, we make better choices.

Meditation is a beautiful thing, yet a lot of people try it and give up on it because it's a discipline. It is one of the strongest disciplines there is, because we're disciplining our body, our mind and our emotions, and at first that's not easy to do.

Also, it may sound rather daunting or even impossible to go from anger, irritation or avoiding being with ourselves to an understanding of our own truth as a loving being. Don't worry; it took me six months, maybe longer, to get the little irritants out of the way, and to go beyond the restlessness of the body and the thoughts that came flooding in, and really begin to experience this expansiveness. It will take time. But we will get little glimmers early on to encourage us to keep going – little moments of insight that come with a high. It's still peaceful, but it's a bigger high than we might get from alcohol or any drug. I've had some incredible highs. I've sat in a golden glowing globe feeling 'Wow!'

When we get that feeling, we want to have it all the time. And the more we spend calm time with ourselves, the more the feeling grows, and the more immersed in it we become. We begin to see truth and love, and realize that is what we are. We know this is what matters, and we don't want anything else. We only want what is true, what is loving and what is peaceful. And we begin to become a more peaceful and loving person every moment of the day.

So meditation is a doorway to the pure, unstressed, healthy, open, loving, calm person we all are at heart. It's not the practice of meditation itself that counts, it's where meditation takes us, and this will be a journey that's unique to every one of us.

Meditation can range from just sitting somewhere quietly right through to mastering complex disciplines and routines that raise our consciousness to a higher level. It's not about wearing white clothes, lighting candles or listening to panpipes – I've found simple ways to have meditation in my life without any formal rituals at all – although, of course, we can do whatever helps us to feel peaceful. Some people write as a form of meditation, 'journaling' or keeping a diary of thoughts. To be honest, I'm totally disorganized in that way. I don't keep diaries, and I've never listened to music to help myself meditate either, but if music helps you initially, go with it. For some people, music can be the way straight to the heart. For me, it is better to have nothing at all. If you were out in the wilderness, you wouldn't have music or any other aids – you'd want to be able to meditate without anything. But please don't think I'm being dogmatic here. I'm not saying that my way is right for everybody, I'm only saying that this is what has been right for me.

My technique, below, is very simple. This is my core practice. I give other versions of it in this book, too, to show how you might apply it in different situations (*see 'One Breath for Calm'*, page 38, *and 'Give Yourself a "Peace Bleep"'*, page 85). If it helps you, that's great, and if not, that's fine too; you will find your own way.

OPENING THE DOOR

This meditation is 'time out', a tea break from life that helps you to keep the outside world out and just 'be' in the present moment. It trains you to think about what you want to think about. It might not be easy at first, but it will become your friend if you persevere. It will be the first thing you turn to in times of stress, or on receiving bad news, or whenever you need to feel at peace.

To begin with, just try this technique for five minutes twice a day, morning and evening. As you feel more comfortable with it, you can extend the time to 10 minutes each session and let it develop from there. Eventually, you'll find that your meditation practice begins to merge naturally into your life.

How do you begin?

Finding Your Place

Finding the right place to meditate helps your practice tremendously. So, where do you feel at peace? This might be a corner of your home or a place in your garden. It might be sitting on the loo if that's the only quiet place in a busy house! I don't know where that place might be for you, but find it! It needs to be somewhere where no one can come rushing in and where there won't be phone calls. Wherever it is, go to the same place every time. If you have a fixed place for meditation, you will find that the minute you walk towards that place, you will begin to feel at peace.

As I write this, I'm in my conservatory, which is my place. The minute I walk in here I feel peaceful, because this is where I meditate, and where I sit and think. It's not a grand room at all. There's lots of light, some small lamp-tables and chairs, and I can see the garden. One of my happiest moments of the day is when I'm up and dressed after breakfast and take a latte and walk into this conservatory (this is when I'm not working, of course). In that moment I feel totally at one with the world, totally at peace, and it's lovely. That's how we can all be, all the time.

Once you have found your place, find a chair that's comfortable and in which you can sit upright with the soles of your feet on the floor, so there will be no uncomfortable pressure on any part of your body when you're meditating. There are many different positions for meditating, but we're keeping it simple here, and sitting is the best position to begin with. You don't need to sit cross-legged with your finger and thumb touching in a yoga mudra – although of course you can if that suits you. If it doesn't, that's fine. As long as you have your chair and a quiet place, you have all you need to start meditating.

Sitting comfortably, let your hands rest naturally where you want them to be. Say to yourself, 'I have left all my worldly life, concerns and worries outside.'

You have let go of everything. You are free from all the daily demands of life.

Going into Your Heart

* *Turn your attention to your breathing. Don't try to control it, just breathe in and out naturally through your nose. If this is uncomfortable for you, then breathe the way you do normally. However you breathe, try to keep it balanced – not too deep, not too shallow, with a steady rhythm; nice and even.*

  If you like, you can visualize waves, as I did when I first started. Think of gentle waves on the seashore, steady and peaceful, coming in and going out in a rhythmic ebb and flow, and inhale and exhale with that movement.

  Or you can think of something else that makes you feel peaceful – maybe being on holiday, or even slowly drinking a cup of tea. Whatever it is, think quietly about it and keep breathing along with it.

• *Then try to just* be. *As a thought comes into your mind, don't try to stop it, but don't engage with it either. Let it pass through. You can't* not *think, but you can decide what you're going to think about. So go back to thinking about your breathing. (This is how you acquire the discipline of deciding what to think about.)*

Your emotions will start to intrude, too. You may be feeling anxious about something, for example. If so, accept that this is the case, tell yourself that you will deal with it later and go back to concentrating on your breathing.

If your body feels uncomfortable or, say, you have an itch, deal with it if you can, then go back to thinking about your breathing.

• *Feel that you are opening up your heart and going into it.*

Going into your heart from your busy mind is like being in a boat. At first you're in the rapids, but you soon begin to sense beautiful calm water ahead, and then you have moments when you're in that calm water – beautiful moments of peace.

Over time, you will begin to feel a golden glowing light around you. When you begin to feel that sensation, you'll find that you can stay with it for some time. You may see the light or not – if you feel it but don't see anything, that's fine. Just go with the feeling.

If you're always in your head and often feel stressed, you might not recognize this feeling of peace when it comes. You might interrupt yourself when you're trying to get into your heart, thinking, Am I doing this right? *And the anxiety may continue as you doubt what's happening. But peace is our natural state of being – it's just that we tend to forget it. So you have experienced it before. You just need to get back to it – to remember who you are.*

When you do begin to feel that peace, that warm glow, you can say to yourself, 'This is how it's meant to be. This is the truth and the way.'

Continuing Your Practice

Over time, you may find that breathing with the waves ceases to be helpful. This can be because the image has become too familiar.

If this is your experience:

- *Next time you begin meditating, really look at the waves and listen to them. Go closer to them.*

- *Then look up from the waves to the beach. See the beautiful white sand there.*

- *Then walk along the beach. Is it empty or are there other people there? You are the observer. Don't have expectations. If there's nothing on the beach, that's fine, just observe it.*

It will take quite a while to get to this point, but you are now in control of what you think and what you see. This will help you in your daily life.

Don't worry if you feel that you are making only a little progress to start with. Meditation is a discipline and can take some considerable time to get used to. But as you continue, you will become accustomed to what you are doing and the intrusions of your thoughts and emotions will become less frequent and then cease altogether. Just keep practising and let go of any expectations. Give yourself regular meditation time and you will naturally progress at your own pace. As I became used to meditating, I would try it twice a day for an hour, and eventually I could sit for three hours. Of course, that isn't for everyone. Now I find that I don't need to set aside meditation time, and in a sense I don't actually have a meditation practice, because that feeling of peace and calm comes whenever I need it. I just sit quietly, take a deep breath and feel everything from the heart. It's so lovely and peaceful.

If you persevere, you will begin to get glimmers of that wonderful feeling of peace and joy, too. Eventually you will find that it is there during your day-to-day life. You will naturally get caught up in things from time to time, but very quickly you will be able to go back to that beautiful, loving, truthful, calm place. That's what we all need and that's where we should all be, all the time.

As you develop your practice, you will begin to see life from a bigger perspective, and discover the truth of who you are and why you are here. You will be able to ask the big questions and sense the answers, because knowledge comes from within. You just need to ask and listen.

Let go of everything, everything, and just be. Now you are your true self.

CONTEMPLATE LOVE

There's a difference between meditating and contemplating. In meditation, you're just being and observing. In contemplating, you're pondering on something, but you need to be wary of the mind taking over. Instead, you can think with your heart.

Having a very deep, wide theme is a wonderful focus for contemplation, because this stops the mind getting hooked on detail when you want to be going into your calm heart. So you might choose to contemplate love, or truth, or the source of All That Is – the big things!

How do you do it?

- *Go into your heart (see page 26). Feel that peace and let it radiate out around you.*

- *Think with your heart by feeling your way into the theme that you have chosen. You'll find that you go into a wider and wider, bigger and bigger picture.*

- *When you feel this huge picture, you'll know that we're all part of it. We're all one. There is only one energy from which we're all created, and that energy is love.*

Everyday Peace

Our primary job is to make peace within ourselves, to be peaceful people. Meditation and loving calmness can take us to inner peace and thereby actually contribute to world peace. Aggressive, angry people do not have peace in their hearts, even if they claim they are fighting for peace. Actually, the people who are making a contribution to world peace usually do so without saying a word to anyone.

When we have peace in our heart, people might say, 'Why is it you're so peaceful?' Then we can talk about it and help them come to that same realization. At that point, we're really making a contribution. But our first contribution is the realization of ourselves as peaceful, loving beings. Of course, we will have our concerns, such as work and family, but ultimately, our only responsibility in life is to ourselves, to make sure we are a peaceful, loving person who lives by the truth. When we do this, we live with our whole being – our soul, our spirit – and find that our approach to life changes for the better.

Until we live this way, we often try to avoid being with ourselves – feeling our feelings, knowing our own truth, whatever that may be. Until I began meditating, I suppose I was one of those people who would have that

Thursday-night panic, thinking, *I've only got five things fixed up this weekend, and what am I going to do the rest of the time?* Now I'm just the opposite – my perfect weekend is having nobody to see and nothing whatsoever to do. I love that. Since Sara's passing, I have lived alone. Yet I still welcome the prospect of an 'empty' weekend that for me feels full because I go within. That's where I find truth, love and peace.

Until we face ourselves, nothing else can ever come right; it's no good searching outwards for health or happiness. Expensive holidays, massage treatments or a packed social diary won't provide true fulfilment. For that, we need to go within. All the things we really want are in our own heart.

Meditation is an exercise; it doesn't make the discoveries for us. But through meditation, or simply by finding a calm moment in our day, we can go within, have a good look at ourselves and start to let go of everything else and just *be*.

Now you might fear this to some degree and think, *If I let go, everything will fall apart*, but if you let go, you'll actually be better able to deal with everything. When you can just *be*, you can be your true self – a powerful, loving and harmonious person. This is who we really are. We are already perfect, we have just forgotten.

Imagine this. You're walking your dog, driving to work or shopping, and you're tense: you're thinking about the nasty neighbour who's arguing about the wall between your property and his. It's bothering you, so, rather than continue feeling angry and resentful, you just stop for a few seconds. You decide to be grateful for this wonderful moment – after all, you're walking your dog, it's not raining and you're not working. You take a breath, go into your heart and allow yourself to go back to the simple truth of who and what you are – a beautiful, powerful being of love.

As you do so, you realize that any aggression, fear or negativity you've been feeling is something that you've allowed in. You've allowed it to bother you. And when you realize this, you find you can just let go of the anger. And you can forgive your neighbour, because he's hurting too. That's why he's behaving that way.

Then you think, *This thing just needs to be sorted*, and a great new feeling flows into the situation. You pour love into it.

When you meet your neighbour again, he's different. The situation is still there, but your attitude to it has changed, and you get a better result because you've sent out that forgiveness, that love.

You can apply this to any difficult situation with another person. Rather than think, *I can't let them get away with this*, and all those sorts of things, just stop. Send them love and forgiveness – and by this, I mean generate these feelings from your heart. People who are angry and aggressive and violent are hurting, and they need a lot of love – even more love than other people. Even the most aggressive person is just presenting a hard exterior that their ego has built up; inside they are a loving, beautiful, calm being who needs to be liberated.

One of the key benefits of a calm, loving and forgiving attitude is that we become aware of how we're responding to people and situations and are able to deal with them in a calmer, more loving way.

Of course, the human condition is a tricky one. We are terribly and perfectly flawed. By 'perfectly flawed', I mean we are perfect beings who have come into a vehicle perfectly designed with 'flaws' to take us through situations that we believe are real and from which we can learn. Some of these situations are very difficult. But through sending out love and forgiveness, I have certainly become much happier and healthier than I ever used to be. I can still slip into stress and problems and get caught up in things, but I am more aware of what's happening now and know I can go into that place of peace within.

I remember having an argument once with a relative who was being particularly difficult and, I thought, quite vicious. I could feel myself getting angry, and I thought, *I don't think I can forgive you for that*, but then suddenly I had a different thought: *No, no, this is all wrong*. And I went into my heart and said, 'I forgive you totally. I send you lots of love and we will resolve this.' And the next time we met, it was over almost in an instant and I realized that our relationship had improved because I had stopped and sent love and forgiveness.

With love and forgiveness, things do get easier, even when life throws you an unexpected challenge. I got in my Volvo once and drove to a shop just around the corner from my home. I jumped out and nipped in to pick up an item, and when I came out, my car had gone. As I was so close to the shop, I'd left the keys in it – and of course, if you've left your keys in your car, your insurance doesn't apply. After I got over the shock and was in a better frame of mind, I thought, *The person who's stolen the car is not living a good life, so I wish them well and hope they will learn from this experience and will sort themselves out*.

A few months later I got a call from the police to say my car had been found and was in a pound in Birmingham. When I went to the pound, I saw a row of battered and bashed cars, and at the end, gleaming, clean and in perfect condition, was mine. So I got my car back in better condition than I'd left it in.

When we practise avoiding blame and sending forgiveness, we eventually get to the point where it's almost a habit. The minute we feel anxious or insecure, *whoomph* – we just go into that place of calm.

I remember one incident when I consciously had to make that head-to-heart shift. I had been made a member of the board of directors for a company going for a television franchise, and sitting with all those businessmen with sharp brains, all talking in technical terms, I felt really inadequate. I felt I had to impress and started thinking, *I've got to show I can do this.* But I felt so uncomfortable that I just stopped and went back into myself, and then the correct thoughts started to come in: *You're here because of your own particular expertise and you don't have to compete with them.* I suddenly felt at peace and could think more clearly.

In the early days of *Coronation Street* I used to step behind the set when I needed to go into the calmness of my heart. Now I do it on the spot with people around me, as long as they're not talking to me. Partly this is practice and partly it's necessity – we no longer have rehearsals and everything is done pretty quickly, especially now that the Street has gone up to six episodes a week. When I acted with my son Linus for the fiftieth anniversary of the show, he couldn't believe how our scene together in the Rovers was done and dusted in five minutes – he'd been in *Law and Order* in the USA for three years and was used to many retakes.

Most of the time the pace of filming is fine, and if I'm honest, I prefer it that way – before, we used to rehearse and then do it live. But if I do get too much in my head, I know I can go into my heart whenever I need to – it's the remedy that gets me instantly back on track.

Here's how you can do it, too.

One Breath for Calm

You can step away from stress and go back into your heart at any time, no matter where you are. Of course, it's ideal if you can sit somewhere quietly when you need to deal with stress, but often this isn't possible. You might be involved in a stressful conversation with another person or be at odds with yourself. You might be in your car, on a train or in a crowded place. If you're feeling inadequate or uncertain, as I did in that business meeting, here's what to do:

- *Just stop for a minute.*

- *Acknowledge that you're in your head, not your heart, and you want to stop thinking, go into your heart and start feeling.*

- *Take a deep breath and go there (see page 26). Feel your energy collecting in your heart and glowing like a big shining sun. Feel the peace. The heart is about feeling, not thinking.*

- *Allow yourself to go into the bigger, calmer picture.*

- *Feel the wholeness of which we're all a part. Feel the peace and love.*

- *Relax and allow these to guide you towards a better decision or performance, a better conversation and more loving thoughts.*

The important thing for me is that through bringing the calmness and love I find in my heart into my everyday life, I am able to manage stress, live well and remain in touch with my true self, as will you. Yes, you will!

SUMMARY: MANAGING STRESS AS
A FIRST STEP TO WELLBEING

- Try five minutes or so of meditation twice a day, morning and evening. You don't have to call it 'meditation' if you don't want to – you can call it 'going within', 'going into your heart' or just 'five minutes of peace', if you prefer. Think of it as a simple way to de-stress and be your authentic self, whatever's going on around you.

- Make peace a priority. Try to avoid blaming others and send out love and forgiveness in any situation that's bothering you. Let go of anger, because anger festers and stops you knowing what you need to know about life and yourself. Although sometimes anger can be a good driving force, in moderation.

- See the bigger picture. This helps you stop obsessing about details.

- Open up to the truth of who you are: a loving, forgiving, intuitive, creative being. You are already perfect.

Chapter 2

DEIRDRE, ANNIE AND SARA: GRIEF AND TRUTH

'Oh, come on, get on with it!'

I could almost hear that throaty laugh, as if Deirdre – or Annie, as she was known to us – were standing right beside me, chivvying me on. There I was, on stage at the 2015 National Television Awards, yet for the first time in my life virtually speechless. My tribute was on the autocue, but I knew this was going to be one of the most difficult things I'd ever been asked to do.

I was saying goodbye to the woman who had been my on-screen wife for 35 years, and it had to be right, just as she would have wanted it. No tears. Annie was a lovely, vital person, and I tried to keep remembering that, and that she herself would have made light of it all. But, like everyone else, I was in shock. Just two days before that tribute, she had passed away.

I had been at her bedside that night, Monday 19 January 2015, along with others close to her. When I'd arrived at the hospital, I'd been told, 'She's lost a lot of weight. Be prepared.'

Annie was frail, but she looked so beautiful – the weight loss had revealed her exquisite bone structure. I know that might be an odd thing to notice at such a moment, but all I could see was her beauty. She was unconscious, sedated with morphine, but she had a glow that seemed to come from within.

I just held her hand. I felt a little tremor run through it and hoped that was a sign she knew I was with her. I wished her well on her journey and thanked her for everything.

'Goodbye, Annie,' I said. 'You know you're going to a beautiful place.'

She was going back home to the spiritual realm and I felt she would be so happy when she got there. And that gave me a great sense of peace.

We'd had no idea she was physically ill, although she'd had many ups and downs – she suffered from depression – and in the last few months she'd started getting more tearful and upset, often sitting outside smoking when we needed to do a scene. I'd go out and comfort her, and when she came back in she would always do the scene brilliantly. But the crying was becoming more frequent, and quite rightly the producers eventually said, 'Look, Annie, you need to go and sort yourself out.' So she agreed to take a three-month break.

She was on anti-depressant medication, and I wondered if it wasn't right for her – maybe she'd outgrown it, given that your body changes as you age. I felt sure that if it was corrected, she'd be back. But that was to be the last time I would work with her.

When I talked about Annie on the night of the National Television Awards in 2016, just a year after her passing, I was heavily criticized for disrespecting her memory. I'd referred to her alcoholism, and her frequent bouts of tears, which had affected filming. But Annie had been so open – she'd laughed about the pills she took, laughed about having been an alcoholic – that when I was talking about her, I felt that same openness. I wasn't telling tales out of school, saying things no one knew about. Everybody knew about her condition – she herself talked about it. She liked talking about it if it helped people.

I don't blame those who criticized my comments. But if something comes at me like that, I have a look at it and

I ask myself, 'Have I been at fault here?' If I think, *Okay, maybe I shouldn't have said that*, I'll say, 'I'm sorry, please forgive me for that,' and move on. Whatever happens, I'll accept the blame if there's some truth in it. If there isn't, I'll let it pass.

Obviously I meant no disrespect to Annie. We were very close and I really did love her. You can understand why actors and actresses quite often have close relationships when they play on-screen partners in a long-running series – they probably spend as much, or even more, time with each other than they do with their real-life wife or husband. Obviously, the sexual side isn't there, but other than that, it's pretty much like a real marriage.

In an ongoing drama, it's very important that you get on with your on-screen partner and your acting styles are similar. I instantly found both with Annie. I met her on the Street in 1972, when she was just 17. She'd only come in for a small part, but the producers instantly saw how good she was, and later they were to discover her brilliant comedy timing. Because of the 16-year age gap, I assumed Annie as Deirdre would be moving around with various on-screen boyfriends. Yet four years after she'd joined us, Ken had a second disastrous marriage and wasn't happy, and they decided to put Ken and Deirdre together. Ken, a so-called intellectual, and Deirdre, a homely girl – there was sure to be some conflict there, and of course there was.

Then there was Deirdre's relationship with Mike Baldwin, whom she'd been involved with before, and the Ken–Mike–Deirdre love triangle hit the pulse of the nation, triggering the first wave of soap columns, soap awards and dedicated soap journalists. The media realized the power of the Street when they flashed up on screen 'Ken and Deirdre United Again!' during a Manchester United game at Old Trafford. The story was front-page headlines. Later, the first wedding of Ken and Deirdre in 1981 got 24 million viewers on ITV – more than the marriage of Charles and Diana two days later!

So Annie and I had lots of wonderful shouting, screaming, emotional scenes, and we could take a scene up, take a scene down, throw it around, and she'd always be there, word-perfect. She was an instinctive, natural actress and had a steel trap of a brain for words. She was lovely to work with and we had a great acting relationship. And you couldn't help but love her – she was always so giving, generous and sensitive. I called her a 'love bomb'. She'd get really upset if someone was going through a hard time. Even if a person just had a headache, she'd dive into her handbag for a painkiller. In fact, her handbag became a big joke. It seemed she had everything in it. If I'd ever wanted a cucumber sandwich, I wouldn't have been surprised if she'd produced a knife, bread, everything.

With Annie, it felt like being married in a parallel life – the life of Ken and Deirdre – even though we'd go our separate ways in the evenings. The vicar who married us on screen, Frank Topping, was actually a Methodist minister in real life.

There were certain similarities in my personal life, too. There were 16 years between Ken and Deirdre, and 17 and a half years between Sara and me. Annie loved cleaning – she'd even put on her gloves and clean the green room between scenes! – and Sara was absolutely fastidious about cleaning and housekeeping. We hired a cleaner when we first moved into our house in Wilmslow, Cheshire, but she was so good with our young children that Sara decided to let her babysit and she'd do the cleaning herself. And so it went on. Every night I'd come back to a beautiful and very organized home.

Annie and I were kindred spirits in many ways. When I was studying astrology, taking a correspondence course from the Faculty of Astrological Studies, she began studying it too, and became quite good at it. I cast her chart for her once, in the early 1990s, and saw that her Venus was going to be conjunct with her Sun. I said, 'It looks as though there's a relationship coming up,' and sure enough, shortly after that David Beckett joined the cast, playing handyman Dave Barton. So Annie and David met, and they were married in 1992.

She also loved to talk about angels and fairies. When Lorna Byrne, an Irish author who sees angels, visited Manchester for a book signing, I took her on a tour around the *Coronation Street* set, and when she looked at Annie, she said, 'She's got two guardian angels.' Most people just have one, but Lorna saw that Annie had one on either side. I felt that was typical of Annie somehow.

I really couldn't have been luckier, being married to Annie as Deirdre in my television life. For 35 years, even when we'd split up, the writers used to regard us as a pair because there was such good chemistry there.

A few weeks after her passing, when we went back on set to the Barlows' living room for the first time, a wave of emotion really hit me. In that room were all the photos of her, all the memories – the things that she'd done, the things that we'd been through there, all the laughter and tears of the

35 years we'd been together. The cast and production crew still feel her presence on set today. She is greatly missed.

***

My wife Sara had died six years before, at just 58 years old. The shock was profound and deep. We used to joke that in my dotage she'd be pushing me round in a wheelchair, and I never imagined for a moment she'd go before me. It wasn't just the years between us; she was so vibrant and beautiful. Coming home from the hospital without her, I felt a huge wave of grief.

I adored Sara, and admired her too. She organized everything for me – I even used to call her 'head girl'! She had been an actress in our early years together and had given that up to support me. For Sara, family came first. She was incredibly close to our two children, Will and Verity, and together we had such a close, loving bond.

Just days before she died, we'd been to lunch with my manager, John Hayes, near his offices in Loughborough, Leicestershire. The three of us had spent five or six hours together, having a great catch-up and talking about future plans. In those plans, we'd always talked about what would happen when I went – never Sara.

Her passing happened so suddenly. It was a normal Saturday morning and we were just chatting, sitting up side by side in bed, when she froze mid-conversation and leaned forwards with an 'oh'. Not a gasp of pain; just a gentle 'oh', like a sigh. Then she fell to the side and lost consciousness. I thought she had fainted. After all, she'd never had a day's real illness in her life.

Although she was rushed to hospital, the doctor pretty well verified that she had died at that moment. I hadn't known that at the time – they'd just got a mask on her, got her on a stretcher and got her to the hospital. They tried everything, but she had already gone. She had died that moment in bed, beside me.

When I saw her again, she looked so serene. I knew her spirit had departed and would already be in the spiritual realm, so, touching her hand, I just said, 'Goodbye, love,' knowing we would meet again someday.

On reflection, I feel that that 'oh', her last utterance, was her spirit, her life-force, departing. She was going back home. It was the most beautiful way to go.

I also feel that Sara chose the moment of her passing. Her soul, her true self, had made that decision. She was a glamorous, beautiful woman, and she decided to go when she was still glamorous and beautiful. She didn't like getting old physically; she was fighting it. Also, she wasn't happy before she went. She'd been in the process of looking back at her life and feeling she had wasted it. I think she was regretting she hadn't done more with her career. The way she went, so peacefully and quickly, was right for her, and the time was right too.

The things that were affecting Sara at that time are part of a negative belief system that is very widespread: the belief that things will only get worse as we age. We can decline at any age if we give in to this collective belief – after all, Sara was only 58 and there was nothing wrong with her. The doctors at first couldn't understand why her heart had just stopped beating, as this is usually due to some illness or abnormality, but there was none in Sara's case. That's why it took us six months to get her death certificate – they wanted to investigate fully why she had died.

The truth is she had died because her soul chose to. We all go when our soul decides we've done enough and it's time to go home. If we're meant to go, we will. If we're not meant to go, whatever happens to us, we won't. Look at Stephen Hawking: he was given two years to live after being diagnosed with motor neurone disease. Yet this brilliant theoretical physicist kept going strong for a further fifty-five years. He was making a vital contribution to humanity, so his soul kept him here.

> **We come here by choice for a purpose and a time. When we die, we return to the heavenly realms to continue as our eternal self, or essence.**

Going back home, what we call 'dying', means returning to the heavenly realms. Dying is only a change of environment. We're all eternal beings who come here to experience separation from 'home' so that we may discover ourselves. We don't need to come here. We come by choice – to learn, to grow and to express who we are. This life is a schoolroom. It is a temporary place, whereas 'home' is our eternal home; it's more alive and active than here. When we're there, we're certainly not sitting on a cloud playing a harp! There are schools of learning there, and we have free will, just as we do here, so we can continue to learn in our own way. And of course everything is made of the one energy, which is love.

I've known this for a very long time, and there are many people out there who know it too. You may be one of them. You may know in your heart that life goes on after 'death', and therefore love goes on too. I send Sara love. Rather than continue to grieve and feel sad, I just send her love. All our loved ones who have passed over and gone to the heavenly realms can feel the love we send them. Love is a permanent connection. Send love to your loved ones who have passed – they pick that up; they know. The communication between you always goes on.

What's interesting here is that science is rapidly catching up with this knowledge. Sir Roger Penrose, a mathematical physicist at Oxford University, and Dr Stuart Hameroff, Director of Consciousness Studies at the University of Arizona, have proposed a Quantum Theory of Consciousness that suggests the soul exists in micro-tubules, which are protein structures inside the brain's neurons. Dr Hameroff explains, 'It's possible that this quantum information can exist outside the body, perhaps indefinitely, as a soul.' The information in the micro-tubules can't actually be destroyed, so survives human death and is dissipated into the universe. This could be seen as the soul going home – returning to Source. Scientists are always trying to interpret creation, and they are getting nearer and nearer to the truth.

As I understand it, when the soul does go home, it goes to the level of its worth. There's no such thing as heaven and hell, but if you're an angry, violent, vicious person, you'll be drawn to that level, and if you're a very loving, kind person, like Annie was, you'll be drawn to that level. Like attracts like. Most of us are going somewhere in the middle. Yet regardless of the level we are drawn to, our true home is a heck of a lot better than here on Earth, and it is eternal.

I'm sure that when Annie and Sara went home, they went to a beautiful, loving place. That's how it should be, and how it is.

My first experience of this truth came way back, through a friend of mine in the army. He told me that his mother was dying in hospital and asked if I would visit her. I'd met her a few times previously. When I arrived, she was lying there with her eyes closed, but suddenly she looked at me, and her eyes had the most beautiful glow. And the look she gave me was a look of sympathy. *She* was actually feeling sorry for *me*. Most people would have thought it would be the other way around, but it wasn't, because she was going home and I was staying here.

When my father was dying, my sister, Beryl, and I had a similar experience. We knew he was close to the end of his physical life and we were each holding one of his hands. Suddenly his eyes opened, and I'd never seen them look so beautiful, almost childlike. He turned to me and then to Beryl, and I saw again that amazing glow – as if he was already seeing the beautiful environment he was about to go to.

Of course, I grieved for Annie, for my father and for Sara. But I tried not to grieve for too long. Grieving for too long can become an indulgent thing. I know that sounds awful. Some people have a lifelong partner, and when that person dies, understandably they may grieve for the rest of their life. I can understand that. Sara and I were married for 31 years – we had one of the longest marriages in show business. We all have our personal grief, but grief and pain can be a place we visit sometimes, but not too often. In time, we can start to remember the happy times we had with that person, enjoy those memories and be grateful for those times. And then just knowing that our loved ones are home, that they are happy and that all is well is enough to ease our pain.

***

I've often wondered if meeting Annie and Sara was part of a plan, because I feel there are certain incidents that are preordained in our lives. Whether meeting my screen wife and real-life wife were such instances, I don't know for certain, but I do know that we feel a sense of recognition with some people and we resonate with them. Like attracts like. There are people who are drawn to us and we are drawn to people of a similar mind.

Sara told me that she knew she would marry me when we first met at a charity event. Of course she didn't tell me that night! But she just knew we'd be together, even given the age difference. She was 22 at the time, and I was 39. I did say to her, 'I'm nearly 40,' but she said, 'What the heck! You don't look it.'

What's important here is that we can all grow to recognize this feeling of connection, of oneness, in a day-to-day way. And it's a simple, natural thing. As humans, we try to make everything complicated, but the truth is simply this: we are all eternal beings and we are all part of one loving energy. Animals, plants, everything that exists comes from one loving Source.

Seeking Truth

We have free will, of course, and it is our choice what we do in this life, but to me it seems obvious that the thing to do is to look for truth. Surely that makes sense. I have always wanted to know what is true. And to search for truth takes effort – we need to go on that journey, to strike out and seek it for ourselves.

As human beings, we are error-making beings; we're perfectly flawed, and we react and respond to the things around us. So it's a very small version of life that we're usually experiencing. We're building up our own philosophy and our own understanding through our environment, through people who tell us things and people we trust. So this search for truth can be very difficult. Yet when we find a truth, we cannot be moved from it; we know it with our heart and soul and our whole being.

Truth is not a belief. I've always had difficulty with the word 'belief'. I might say I believe something, but I say it in an agnostic way, meaning I'm not sure about it. It may be so, or it may not; it certainly isn't a truth. Beliefs can change. They change because they're not the truth. The truth never changes. The truth is the truth, and will never let us down.

The place to look for truth is inside ourselves – it is an inward journey. The reason we can look inside ourselves for answers is because, as part of the loving Source, we know everything; we're all connected with the whole, and to the collective experiences of all our incarnations on Earth. In our true selves, we are the sum total of all that we have been, and we are also the wisdom of our soul. Of course we have to deal with the modern world – live as human beings, earn a living, and so on. Yet we can do that *and* be in touch with our true selves and the knowledge within.

To feel this connection and access our true wisdom, we need to go inwards and listen to our heart.

TRUTH AND KNOWING

Experiencing truth is a feeling of knowing, a resonating. The minute you hear a truth, you will resonate with it. You might read a line in a book and feel a 'Yes!', or hear a song that feels so perfect you're almost vibrating with it. This is the wisdom of your soul, which existed before all your lifetimes.

That moment of resonance came for me when I read the line: 'Being one with the infinite.' I felt excited; I felt a oneness with the infinite, because it reminded me of my own knowing.

When you resonate with a thought, a lyric, with words, with anything, you *know* it is true. You can't prove it to anyone else, as your path to truth is an individual journey.

It is your truth, it is where you are and it is the place from which you grow. And the more open and aware you are of the knowledge you already possess, the more these experiences will come.

Some of this soul wisdom, along with the wisdom acquired over incarnations, will come in as little thoughts. This is your true self talking to you. Rather than just let these thoughts pass, pause for a moment and consider: *Where did that come from? How do I know this? Why do I recognize that person?*

Ask for truth, ask for understanding, ask for help to be who you are. If you ask, you will find the answers.

If you want to know the truth about anything, say, 'Please help me,' to the universe, or your own word for the creator, and you will find that guidance will cross your path, maybe as a news item on television, a statement or a saying. It's quite amazing. The minute you start to look for what is true, you receive tremendous help.

Your soul actually knows everything already. It has learned a lot from incarnations, but incarnations are not the only source of wisdom. You don't need to get into who you were in a past life, thinking, *Maybe I was a king, or Cleopatra.* You don't need to know who you were; you only need to know your true self, your eternal self, your spiritual self, your essence. These words all mean the same thing. Once you understand your own truth and resonate with it, you will trust the guidance that comes from within.

Truth comes more readily to you then, because you see it everywhere. You live more harmoniously as a physical and spiritual being. You begin to sense your life purpose. You become more accepting, more allowing and more forgiving, which raises your consciousness, so you live a better life, a happier life and a longer life.

Once you understand that we're all part of one energy, then you understand that to harm another is to harm yourself. So you begin to work to bring world peace.

Over the years, I've realized that truth and love are the only things that matter. And when you live in harmony with truth and love, of course, peace and forgiveness come naturally to you.

That night on stage, waiting to give Annie's tribute speech, so much of what I've been telling you about her flashed through my mind: the years we'd been together, her vitality and kindness, how we'd been soul mates on-screen as husband and wife, and off-screen as close friends and colleagues. Knowing Annie is in a beautiful, happy place now, free of pain, kept me calm. We had talked at length about spiritual matters, and she knew, too, that beyond the life of the physical body there is only love.

I could feel Annie's presence in that room as I spoke those words to her relatives, her beloved husband and her *Coronation Street* family. On stage, they'd projected a picture of her, smiling and beautiful. And when I finished my short speech with 'I love you, Anne,' I could almost see her wrapped in the love that she so freely gave to everyone she knew.

Chapter 3

LOVE, FORGIVENESS AND WELLBEING

To live a long, healthy and happy life there is one thing we should seek above all else. All the exercise, diets and lifestyle teachings in the world will only have short-term and minimal effects without this. What is it? Living in a way that is true to our nature.

This is profound, and may sound complicated and difficult. But actually, so like many truths, it is simple.

Our nature is love. We are all beings of love. We can express this love through forgiveness, kindness, compassion and gratitude. But, because we are perfectly flawed, we are mostly at some distance from this. Many of us have completely forgotten our true nature. What we can all do is to place our feet firmly on the path to remembrance and get as close as we can to our true selves: to love.

Love

Do You Love Yourself?

Our natural state is one of love. We were made with love. We were made by love, we were made of love, so our natural state is *to* love. And we need to love ourselves first of all. Only this can bring us wellbeing and happiness.

Do you love yourself? If you've ever felt that you don't, what you're saying is that you don't know yourself – your true, already perfect eternal self. It's easy to love yourself once you know who you truly are, not the personality you think you are.

If you've ever said, 'I don't *like* myself,' what you've actually meant is 'I don't like a lot of the persona I've built up.' We build things up in our heads – philosophies and ideas of living – and these are created by the ego. The ego is the personality that we have created with our mind, emotions and free will. Have a good look at your ego. It will have a lot of positives, as human nature is fundamentally good, but too much ego, with misguided desires, can create havoc in the world.

As children, we come into this world seeing angels and beautiful things. We naturally have enthusiasm and a love of life. Yet this can get knocked out of us as we grow up, so we don't remember all the beautiful things and we inhibit that joy. We get overly attached to earthly things, too, and protect what we think. We identify with the ego and lose who we truly are.

At one point in my career, this became an issue for me. When I was first studying with Dr Maugham, I considered giving up acting altogether because acting can be an ego-driven profession and I couldn't understand how it could be compatible with what I was learning about life. I wondered if I could withstand Ken and the emotional helter-skelter he had to go through – after all, he was a kind of alter-ego.

In many ways we are very dissimilar. I'm pretty peaceful, but Ken gets angry. I was happily married for 31 years and have been in a job I love for even longer, but Ken's been in and out of marriages and jobs all his life. It could have been problematic, but I've realized that what he does is give me a safe experience of emotions I don't usually have. When he's having a row, I can get angry and quite enjoy it and think, *Hey, yeah, this is quite fun, isn't it?*

It works because the cast are all together in this – we're all friends and we know it's all okay. The studio and set are happy and relaxed, and there are no big divas. (If anyone's entitled to be a diva it's me, anyway, as I'm the senior member of the cast!) And because we're in the controlled environment of the set, I can leave Ken there at the end of a day's filming.

Now I might be able to do this, but it can be different for viewers. Our storylines can evoke a powerful response in people and touch their lives. I was dropping off Verity at school one day and another child came up to talk to her, but suddenly her mother shouted, 'Get away from that man!' Ken was having one of his affairs at the time. Later he really had his comeuppance and lost Deirdre. Three years later, the same mother actually came up to me and said, 'You know I really hated you, because that's exactly what happened to me. But I saw how it worked out and watching you really helped me.'

We often don't realize how connected we are to other people. But when we truly love ourselves, we don't often feel lonely. In reality, we are never alone. We all have people around us all the time; we're all connected to one another and to Source and the universe. And we're all loved and protected by the universe, by our guardian angels and by other beings. We are at one with everyone and in tune with the universe itself.

I remember once feeling very alone and sorry for myself and asking to feel the love of Source. Then, walking along the street, I saw a mother with a baby looking happy, and I suddenly felt a tremendous love for them – so much love that I wanted to cry. I had the full realization that if you love, you draw love to you. Thoughts are energy, and whatever you think, you get back. So, instead of thinking *Nobody loves me* or *I want to be loved*, get out there and open up to love. It's everywhere. Love the world, love the Source of all of it, love everybody, and then *whoomph* – back it comes to you! Love changes the situation instantly.

So now, whenever I'm beginning to feel irritated by anything, I just send loving thoughts to everyone involved. If I'm in a crowded, noisy room and begin to feel annoyed because I can't hear properly, I just stop. (I have some hearing loss, which has affected me for many years; it's the result of an accident that happened when I was in the army.) I take a deep breath, go into my heart and then send love by sending the thought *I love you all*, and suddenly I feel calm and a part of everything. I feel a connection with everyone, whether I know them or not. Not being able to hear them can still be a bit irritating – but of course, we're not perfect!

Forgiveness

This ties in with forgiveness. Let's talk about that now.

Self-forgiveness

One of the most important things is to forgive ourselves, totally and absolutely. When we forgive and love ourselves, we can forgive and love others.

In life we have experiences that are there to help us realize that we are, by nature, beautiful forgiving beings. Life is really just about remembering who we truly are. It is that simple.

We forget who we are much of the time – the world is so busy and stressful, and we're often living in the mind, pulled this way and that and doing things that aren't quite right. We can't help that. We're flawed, perfectly flawed, as I mentioned earlier. We are designed that way in order to learn.

We're all really learning the same lesson: how to remember our true and loving nature. Our soul purpose presents us with certain experiences that are designed to show us how to do this. So we need to love ourselves with *all* our imperfections. They are all part of our soul's plan.

We come into this life through a veil of forgetfulness and our circumstances will condition us. But our conscience is always there to guide us and tell us when we're doing things wrong. Of course we'll still make mistakes, which is where self-forgiveness comes in. Self-forgiveness helps us to look after ourselves more and be kinder to ourselves.

| Kindness is love in action.

If we need forgiveness for something, we need to look at it and accept what was wrong and take steps to see that it doesn't happen again, so in a sense forgiveness does need to be earned, even though it's always given. Source, the universal life-force, always forgives us. Source is like the father of a family who loves all his children but doesn't like how a lot of them behave!

We can begin with forgiving ourselves in small, everyday ways. Say you go out of your front gate and a cyclist nearly knocks you over and swears at you and you want to swear back. This is typical of the way we just react to external stimuli and maybe don't behave as well as we should. These little events are happening around us all the time.

When something like this happens to me I look at the situation and, however awful I think someone else has been, I try to see where I may have contributed to it. If I think, *Maybe I wasn't very kind*, in my mind I send love to the person and ask their forgiveness.

When I've finished looking at the circumstances and sending love, I just say to myself, 'Well, that's me, imperfect, as are we all, but yes, of course I forgive myself, just as I am forgiven for everything I do.'

If this applies to you, whatever's happened, just have a look at how you might have contributed to it and what little area in yourself might be improved, and make sure you put that bit right. Then send love to the other person and ask for their forgiveness.

I know this is an everyday example, dealing with one of the many irritations that cross our path. But the need for self-forgiveness is the same when dealing with very serious situations – when we made a decision that had severe consequences, for example, or felt guilt after a traumatic event, even though it couldn't be helped.

When our daughter Edwina died at just 18 months, Sara and I felt terrible guilt, even though we knew there was nothing we could have done to save her. We couldn't have known that the infection that started with a cold would take her life. We went through every tiny detail of what happened on that terrible night of 16 November 1984, trying to understand how she had been fine one moment, then just 30 minutes later had died in her cot. Your children aren't supposed to die before you. And we were the responsible parents – responsible for our beautiful girl's wellbeing, her development, her happiness.

Over many, many months, we had to learn to forgive ourselves for not being able to save her. It was a terribly hard thing to do, so when I say we should forgive ourselves, I don't say it lightly at all. I know it can be extremely difficult, but it's the only way. If we don't forgive ourselves, we can't love ourselves and be loving to others. When Edwina died, our other daughter, Verity, was just three years old. If Sara and I had retreated into recrimination and self-loathing, what could we have offered each other or our very young daughter who had just lost her sister? We needed to be able to keep loving each other and give Verity all the love she needed, too.

Forgiving Others

There are several myths about forgiving others. It doesn't mean you forget what has been done to you or that you have to be friendly towards the perpetrator, or anything like that. It doesn't mean that they will get away with it. We live under the law of cause and effect, so they will have to come to terms with what they have done and go through whatever process is right for them to understand the consequences of their actions. This is a 'process' – it's never punishment, it's always a teaching.

If a person has done something wrong, it is because they have strayed away from who they are, because they really are something beautiful. Instead of condemning them as a bad person, say, 'That person needs a lot of love.' The more aggressive and horrible a person is, the more love they need, so always, in whatever judgement you happen to come to (and we can't help it, we make judgements all the time), remember that the people who are doing the worst things are the ones who are hurting the most.

That's not easy, particularly if they've been extremely aggressive towards you or someone you care about; I understand that. It's extremely hard. Learning to forgive might be a lifetime lesson, but forgiveness ultimately releases you. It's part of the letting-go process that we all need to go through to get away from some of the ego we've built up and into the truth, reality and love of who we are.

Because we are part of the energy of Source, which is love, and that energy is forgiving, it is in our nature to forgive. If we don't forgive, we're going against our own nature.

This can make us feel unhappy, bitter and resentful. So forgiving others doesn't alter in any way their situation, but it does alter ours. Once we forgive them, we are free.

> **An act of forgiveness is an act of love. When you forgive, you liberate yourself.**

Anger and Pride

I had a big lesson back in the early 1990s that involved forgiveness, along with anger and pride. When people get angry, they often feel righteous indignation as well, because they believe a situation needs to be put right. They may think they're not getting across their point of view, or they're being got at. Whatever the situation, if someone's angry, it's because they're fearful of losing something. This describes me perfectly back then.

In November 1990, *The Sun* newspaper published a story about me that was not true and was very unkind. It was hard not to feel angry. I was bewildered and frustrated, and took them to court in 1991. Even though I won damages of £50,000, because that was the same sum the newspaper had offered me as an out-of-court settlement, I became liable for all the court costs. If the jury had known this, maybe they'd have offered £50,001 and I wouldn't have been liable for costs at all. But they didn't and I was, and I took that up with my solicitors at the time, because I felt I'd been ill-advised. And the legal bills mounted up and up, until in 1999 I had to declare bankruptcy. Sara and I found ourselves owing around £600,000.

I'd been very hurt by what had been printed and I thought I wanted justice, but now I realize that it was about pride and ego. And all that led to was sky-high legal bills and so much pressure for Sara and me that I ended up with a burst ulcer, and Sara had a migraine so severe she was blind for two days.

It was a lesson for me – a lesson in pride and a lesson in forgiveness. I'd actually had the chance to forgive Ken Irwin, the *Sun* reporter who'd written the story, when I'd bumped into him at Euston station queuing for the Manchester train. That was the universe offering me an opportunity to let it go – to see that he was just doing his job and that the story would probably be forgotten in a week or two – but I just couldn't. He said, 'Hello,' and we had a terse exchange that I'm not proud of, which amounted to me saying I'd see him in court. I've had to forgive myself for not taking that opportunity, and forgive myself for the anger I felt, too.

It was a hard lesson and it took years to recover from it financially. But it was my lesson, and I accept that.

We can't change what happens to us, and what happens to us may not be right, but we can change how we respond to it. We can step back from anger and respond with love.

Stepping Back from Anger

If ever you're angry, you just need to step back. Stepping back doesn't necessarily mean you're wrong in what you're trying to do, but there's something within you that isn't wholly connected and isn't coming from a loving, truthful place. So if ever you're angry, however right you may think you are, there's some ingredient that isn't correct. Take a look at yourself and see where that anger is coming from.

People can get very cross when their beliefs are questioned, because it threatens to break their understanding of the cosy little life that they're living. But more often than not, their beliefs need to be challenged. If a belief cannot stand up to questioning, then it's not a truth. And you only want to follow a truth, not a belief. So, when you feel anger and fear, always have a good look at yourself. Somewhere in there you're disconnected from love. Because if you genuinely come from the heart, speaking love and truth, you will always go in the right direction.

Of course it can be extremely difficult to step back from anger when someone has harmed you or a loved one. It's hard to forgive the person responsible, and that is understandable. When this happens, there may be a lesson there about understanding the nature of forgiveness. If a bad experience comes to you, it can be an opportunity to learn, to be more forgiving and loving, and to find and express yourself. For this reason, some people may be destined to go through a traumatic situation because of certain agreements made before incarnating into this life. Life is a school and we are all here to learn, including learning to step back from anger and forgive.

Understanding Anger and Fear

Anger comes from fear, and fear only exists where there is no love. We were given fear for survival reasons only, not as a way of being. It's fear that pumps the adrenaline that gives us the impetus to get away from danger. But while fear is meant to be a part of life, it's now out of control. The majority of people live in fear most of the time.

If you allow fear to seep into your life and you feed it, it quickly takes a hold. Years ago, I had panic attacks, partly because of my fear of death. I couldn't believe there was just oblivion. This may also have been because my father was dealing with death and dying day in, day out. As I mentioned earlier, he was a doctor, as was his father before him. I began studying to be a doctor too, but stopped when I was called up for national service. When I left the army at 25, I decided I wanted to be an actor rather than go back to medicine.

I think my fear of death was exacerbated by seeing my father dealing with all sorts of serious diseases before antibiotics were available, including the polio epidemic before they had the vaccine. Illness was more dangerous then. I also knew my grandfather, Hugh, had died suddenly of flu before I was born, and my grandmother, Mildred, had died of the same illness just three days later. So as a young man, I was really frightened of death. It became a big fear for me, but what it did was make me want to find out what life was about. What was death? Was there an afterlife? What was our purpose here on Earth? So beneath that fear of death was actually a need to find the truth.

In a way, it was a gift.

Once I learned to explore, to find my own spiritual understanding, my fear began to diminish. And then I found people who knew the great truths, such as my teacher, Dr Maugham.

I have no fear of death at all now. On the contrary, death is something we can look forward to, because we'll be going back to our eternal home and will be closer to Source, to love. Of course, it's natural to be worried about dying, because we just don't know how it will happen to us in this life. I just trust that all will be as it is meant to be. I focus on the present and look positively towards the future.

Ironically, I faced that old fear of death again very recently, this time through Ken. The Street's producer, Kate Oates, revealed the latest storyline: he was to have a stroke. My first reaction was, 'Will he live?' because of course I want nothing more than to continue playing Ken for as long as I can.

Playing the part of a stroke victim had its challenges. It had to be medically accurate, so I went to some lengths to make sure I got it right – that I showed the facial paralysis correctly, for example. We had an expert to advise us – Dr Pippa Tyrell. She explained that I wouldn't be able to speak immediately after the stroke, whereas the script had me collapsing and then saying something. I said that what I would like to do was bite my tongue and then try to talk through it. She agreed that this would work, so that's what I did. She was very helpful, and she was with us on set while Ken's stroke scenes were being filmed, as it was vitally important to us that my portrayal was accurate.

When you get it right, it's really enjoyable, acting out something that's entirely realistic. And, I repeat, my old fear of dying is long gone, because of knowing that we're all eternal beings, and when we die, we go to back to our eternal home.

If you have a situation that is very difficult for you, try not to allow fear in. If you do, it can only make matters worse. Fear is only an emotion, and it disappears when faced. You are always protected, you are looked after, and if you look for truth and love, your attempt to solve whatever problem you have will be guided and you'll be helped.

When you have love, and are love, fear cannot exist. So, in any situation, if you feel that fear is coming in, just pour love over it. You don't have to fight fear or join it, or blame yourself for feeling it; just remember who you truly are. You are love, so be it. Live it.

When you live it as much as you can, you start to become healthier and feel happier. You get on better with people, and difficult situations don't seem to come your way so much.

| Fear is a disconnection from love.

It's when we go against who we truly are that we don't feel happy. Sometimes we don't realize we're doing it. But then we might have the feeling that something isn't right. That's our conscience niggling at us. It alerts us when we're doing or being something that isn't true to our nature, and this comes through our feelings. It is our feelings, not our thoughts, that will give us the truth in this situation, and give us the opportunity to reconnect to love.

If the situation continues, however, our disconnection and unhappiness can lead to depression. Left unattended, depression can spiral even deeper, and once we're in a dark tunnel, it's easier to go into the negative, into fear, than be positive and proactive.

If you ever find yourself in a situation like this, just stop and think, *I've forgotten who I am. I am a beautiful, loving being and that is what I want to get back to.* Know this in your heart and start acting and living as a beautiful, truthful, loving being.

Meditation can help us to live without fear and reconnect to love, and, as I said earlier, don't let the word 'meditation' put you off. It's just being quiet and going into the truth in your heart.

There are awful things happening in the world, but we don't need to be fearful about them – we can still go into love and truth and know that at the end of the day love and truth will always win. They cannot be defeated; the darkness will always lose out to the light. Always.

Dealing with Anxiety

Along with anger and fear, anxiety is also widespread in society, and it is also an indication that we are not living true to our nature.

Anxieties come when we let ourselves be drawn into the complexities and minutiae of life. If we are caught up too much in the details, we get distracted and can miss our main goal. It is often necessary to focus on details, but this is only the path to our goal and not the goal itself.

So, keep your main goal in mind when you are dealing with the minutiae. Love always sees the big picture, and if you're seeing it too, you'll deal with the challenges that come your way very easily.

The Buddhist teaching is 'non-attachment'. Try not to be attached to anything. If you become attached to one outcome or focus too much on one thing, then you're denying a lot of other things the opportunity to come your way, and your life is out of balance. When you're attached, you have blinkers on and can't make clear judgements. Unfortunately, that's how many of us live most of the time. But we don't need to.

When we understand the nature of love, we know it isn't partisan, it isn't particular – it includes everybody and everything. (Romantic love is different. It is a version of the great truth that can have some negative aspects to it, like possessiveness, jealousy and being too dependent.) We are free, open and loving beings, and when we're detached, we don't love anyone or anything *less*, we love all things *more*. Detachment is actually a beautiful thing.

When we become less attached to outcomes, it's also easier to take the holistic view, to see the bigger picture. We can take this approach all the time. Rather than think, *I'm in this situation, what am I going to do?*, we can deal with things as if they're slightly away from us – over there, rather than right here. We can think, *Okay, there's that situation there that I will look at and I will deal with, and it will pass anyway.* Or, *If I can't deal with it, I'll let it ride for a while until I can. Meanwhile, I will ask for help.* We don't ask for help enough.

Another way of dealing with anxiety is to take a calm, safe moment out from everything that's going on.

GIVE YOURSELF A 'PEACE BLEEP'

Before I learned about meditation I used to give myself what I called a 'peace bleep' – or 'peace break'. I would take a deep breath, then take some time out and allow a feeling of calm and peace to come over me, even if just for a minute or two. We all need to feel at peace, to have moments during the day when all is well. Inner peace is the key to a relaxed mind and healthy body.

You can take these moments for yourself without any aids – without the tea, without the cigarette – regardless of how manic you think your life is. We tend to look outside for comfort, but the true answer is within ourselves.

Just like a tea break, nothing harmful can happen to you when you're having a 'peace bleep' – it's a calm, safe time out from everything that's going on. You'll come back to the problems later, but you'll be a bit stronger for your few minutes away.

- *Sit somewhere where you won't be disturbed. Rather than browse the Internet for a break from your screen or make a phone call, find a place that is calm and quiet – preferably not your office desk.*

- *Just sit comfortably, close your eyes and leave any problems you have sitting outside the door for the duration of your 'bleep'.*

- *Breathe and just be yourself.*

Eventually, once your inner life becomes more peaceful, calm, loving and caring, this will be reflected in your outer world. Better things will come to you and you'll find that you're better able to deal with life.

Wellbeing

Being Aware

To enjoy real wellbeing, we not only need to love and forgive ourselves, but also to be aware of our true feelings. Then we can deal with them. We might be suppressing fear or anger, for example, as I realized I was when I first began to meditate.

Some people do this in a way that appears positive. They might go out helping other people while actually being quite angry or fearful in their own hearts. Quite often we look outside ourselves for relief from our own worries, when in fact, as I mentioned earlier, the answer is inside.

If we distract ourselves, our worries don't go away. They'll still be there, and there they will stay. We'll only get rid of them by going within and getting ourselves totally at peace, totally calm. Then we'll be able to think clearly and understand the real nature of our worries. And we'll realize that we are a beautiful, perfect, loving, human being, and so is everyone around us.

All we are actually responsible for in life is coming to that understanding and then being the loving, forgiving being that we are. And then people will come to us and say, 'How come you always look so relaxed and so happy and healthy?!'

At that point, we can help them. They will come to us. They won't know why, but they will find themselves confessing to us and wanting to talk to us, because something in them recognizes the love, forgiveness and kindness within us. This is what happens as we develop and become calmer and more loving and balanced.

Being Grateful

Along with forgiveness, love and truth, thankfulness is essential to us in life. This is because gratitude helps things flow to us. This can really help whenever we're feeling low. Negative thoughts can block the good things that are coming, but if we can feel grateful for what we already have, everything will begin to improve.

INVITATION TO EXPANSIVE GRATITUDE

To begin with, try to be grateful every morning. Let this be the first thing that comes to mind when you wake up. Give yourself as much time as you can to do this – I usually spend a few minutes on it, but do what you can.

Give thanks to the creator of All That Is or to the universe:

- *Be thankful for the gift of life. Be grateful that you're alive.*

- *Be grateful for the sun that shines and gives you life, for planet Earth and for all it provides.*

- *Be grateful for all animals, for what they do for you and for just being what they are.*

- *Be grateful for the people, seen and unseen, who love you and look after you.*

- *Be grateful for every little thing you have.*

- *Be grateful for the things that come at you that you may not like. A really bad experience is a big opportunity to learn, understand yourself and get stronger. So embrace it with thanks.*

When you do this, you'll find that soon you won't consciously need to think about being grateful each morning – you will feel it naturally throughout the day. It will be part of everything you do. You'll be grateful for a cup of tea – you'll say 'thank you' whether or not you've made it yourself. If you walk, alone or with a dog, you'll find yourself saying, 'Thank you for this wonderful moment,' as it's happening. You'll recognize the good times and live in the here and now.

Cups of tea and walks aren't the small things in life; they are the big things that put us more in tune with ourselves and with peace and happiness. If you tend to overlook small pleasures, you're missing out. If you get a lovely feeling when you're walking the dog, remember that feeling, retain that feeling, and then you can retain that state of being wherever you are and whatever you're doing.

If you can do this, your life will become more whole and beautiful. And that's how it should be.

Releasing Energy

You can also enhance your wellbeing by getting the energy of life flowing. If you ever feel down and tired, for example, make yourself do something that you've been putting off for a long time. The energy will flow and you will feel liberated.

It's the same with your home. If it's full of clutter you haven't got around to clearing out, or you're behind with paperwork and jobs you've been neglecting, this can have a negative effect on you. Clutter is disorganization and chaos, and if you live in chaos, your thoughts and emotions get chaotic, too.

If your house is overflowing with too much stuff, that's going to affect you every time you walk through the front door. According to feng shui, the art of arranging your environment to encourage positive energy, if you've got a room where you just dump things, there will be negative energy there. All the accumulated rubbish will create it. You know how it feels when you walk onto an empty beach or hillside and get a wonderful sense of openness and freedom? And then you walk into your own little house and your heart sinks. There's damp coming through here, ants coming in there, and the roof still needs repairing... immediately you're depressed.

Undone routine jobs have the same effect, and the longer you leave them, the harder they are to get down to. I used to leave all my correspondence until the day when I would suddenly get the urge to tackle all my admin. And afterwards I'd feel great, thinking, *Wow! Why didn't I do this before?* When you do get down to those neglected jobs, you get a wonderful surge of energy in return.

Getting finances under control comes under that 'routine jobs' heading – or at least, it should do. Many of us avoid dealing with bills or keeping a proper track of spending. We might have a really tidy, clean home, but can't face going through our bank statements. It might be because there's information there we don't want to see, like spending on things we feel guilty about afterwards, or because we're not confident dealing with figures. For some people, not paying attention to financial matters is a kind of self-avoidance – not wanting to look at the reality of where they are. But if you give yourself a regular time to tackle finance each week – say just an hour checking bills and statements and budgeting what you need for the coming weeks – you always feel more in control.

If you have a money problem, a big debt that you cannot repay, do the best you can and then ask the universe for help. We do not ask for help often enough. Ask for abundance; there is enough for everyone. Do your best by looking at why you have the problem, and take steps to avoid it happening again. But keep asking for help.

I'm not brilliantly tidy or meticulous, but I like to know where everything is. Since Sara died, I've had to! My manager, John, helps me with the financial side of things, but Sara was the organizer in our house.

I know it's really about trying to find a balance; if you're over-fastidious, over-neat, always washing and cleaning and constantly putting everything away, you've no time to really live, because you're always trying to meet a demand. I just try to keep on top of my to-do list and stop my home getting too cluttered. I let it be lived in, and I enjoy the time I spend there. It's all about finding a balance.

Finding a balance can be key to so many other aspects of wellbeing, too.

Finding Balance: Laughter

Balance is the heart and head working together; the right measure of thought and feeling that helps us to take the right decisions, see the bigger picture of life and be a loving, forgiving person. We can get a sense of how balanced we are now by looking at how easily we laugh and how often we lose our temper. That really shows whether we're in balance.

I once heard that 'humour is common sense, dancing'. When we can laugh or dance with our thoughts, we're relaxed and our whole being is in harmony. Humour gives us balance, provided it's in the right measure. I do like having fun, and I do send myself up a bit at times. In the 1980s I agreed to help a friend promote his single '*J'aime*, Teddy Bear' and danced and rapped with him on ITV's *Good Morning*. Now I'm a pretty rubbish dancer. In fact, I was awful then, and it was all a bit ridiculous. So that was something to laugh at, but my dancing certainly wasn't common sense! Still, even though I've got very little rhythm (I'd never, ever, do *Strictly* for that reason, though I have great admiration for those who do), and I cringe now if I look back on that, it was certainly fun at the time.

If you can't laugh freely, and you feel you've lost your sense of humour or often lose your temper, it's often a sign that you're focusing on one aspect of life to the exclusion of something else. Try to regain your balance. See the humour in life as much as you can, because it keeps you in harmony with all that is. Angels laugh – they laugh a lot. Learn to laugh at yourself, too; it keeps you centred. I love a good laugh, and we laugh a lot as a family. Sometimes at my jokes!

Cathy Goodman, who is featured in the spiritual film *The Secret*, relates how she was diagnosed with breast cancer. Rather than give in to fear, she believed absolutely in her heart that the cancer did not exist. She says, 'I saw myself as if cancer was never in my body.' Every day, she was thankful for being healed. She did not have chemotherapy or radiotherapy. Instead, she watched comedies like old Charlie Chaplin films and just laughed. Within approximately three months, the cancer had gone.

Of course, I'm not suggesting that anyone with cancer forgoes chemotherapy and/or radiotherapy, as Cathy Goodman chose to do, but research suggests that laughter can play a part in healing cancer and strengthening the immune system. At the School of Medicine at Loma Linda University, California, research led by Dr Lee Berk, a leading scientist on the effects of 'mirthful' laughter on the body, found that watching a one-hour comedy resulted in an increase in the body's natural killer cells. These cells, which seek and destroy cancer cells, also became more active.

Laughter makes us feel good; it lowers stress hormones and, as suggested by researcher Robin Dunbar at Oxford University, it releases endorphins, the brain's feel-good chemicals. A good belly-laugh works out the abdominal muscles and gives us the endorphin release we would get from physical exercise. As the saying goes, 'laughter is medicine' – but of course, with balance and in moderation. Which isn't always easy once you start giggling...

SUMMARY: LOVE, FORGIVENESS AND WELLBEING

- Love yourself, look after yourself and be kind to yourself.

- Be at peace. Forgive yourself for everything you have done and everything you will do. Source always forgives you, so forgive yourself.

- Don't let negative thoughts take charge, blocking the good things. Spend the first few minutes of every day with thoughts of gratitude. You will set yourself up for the day.

- Let go, accept and allow.

- Laugh!

- Live in a way that is true to your nature as a being of love.

Chapter 4

IN COURT

Making my way into a beautiful compartment on an Emirates plane about to depart Dubai, I should have had nothing to worry about. I was flying first class on the final lap of my journey home from Auckland to Manchester. I'd been the narrator of *Corrie!*, a *Coronation Street* play by Jonathan Harvey. We'd just finished a four-city tour of New Zealand and I was looking forward to getting back to Weatherfield.

But just as I was settling myself into my seat, an intense feeling suddenly swept over me: 'Oh – I don't want to go home!' I felt it so strongly, and just couldn't account for it. I loved my home; everything was good. Why should I have that feeling?

It was only afterwards, of course, that I realized why. I was to be arrested three days later.

Just a month before, I'd been hounded by journalists outside the gates of my home in Wilmslow as I'd prepared to leave for New Zealand. I'd recently made some comments on my spiritual understanding in an interview and it had attracted a lot of negative media attention. I'd had such a job getting out of my own front gates that Granada Television had had to send a security guard to help me. Eventually I'd got to the airport and boarded my flight, thinking, *Thank goodness that's over*. But it wasn't.

The press attention continued in New Zealand – not so much from the New Zealand press, but certainly from the British press. As a result, Granada advised me not to give any interviews when I was there, which was a shame, and upsetting for the people wanting to promote the play, so it did create some problems. But I completely accepted Granada's decision, and overall I enjoyed the tour. *Corrie!*, a celebration of the fiftieth anniversary of the Street, had got great reviews in the UK, and our New Zealand fans loved it, too.

***

Back home, the buzzer for my electric gate went at around 8 o'clock on the morning of 1 May 2013. I was still jetlagged, and though the intercom was by the bed, I didn't hear very well what was being said. Thinking it was the postman, I pressed the 'open' button, got out of bed, put my dressing gown on and went downstairs to open the front door.

Five policemen were walking up the drive.

I let them in, and then one of them said, 'We're arresting you,' and went through the charges.

I heard the words as if they were being spoken somewhere in the distance. Shock affects you in funny ways. You go into a sort of unreal mode – that's the only way I can describe it. As the policeman was speaking, the colour seemed to drain from everything and there was a sort of mist around us.

Then they told me two policemen were going to search the house and stay there, two were going to drive me to a police station and one was going stay with me while I got dressed, which he did. He stood in the bedroom watching quietly while I quickly found some clothes.

They took the computers and went through everything in the house. Then they drove me to a police station in Leyland, Lancashire, about 40 miles from my home. By the time I got there, the media knew all about it. I've no idea how they knew. At that point, I'd not even been able to call my family or my manager, because I didn't have my phone with me.

I had no reason to expect anything like that, and it had never entered my mind that it could happen. It was only later that I remembered the feeling I'd had on the Dubai plane – that strange feeling of dread that had no foundation. It was as if my intuition had been telling me something wasn't right.

When I got to the police station, I was still convinced that there was nothing seriously wrong. I thought that once I'd answered their questions, I'd go home and that would be the end of it. The fact that the media were all onto it did make me think, *Oh gosh, this is going to be awful*, but I still thought it would all be over in a little while.

The police said I could make one phone call, but I hadn't got my phone and there was no one at my house. I was on my own and I really didn't know what to do, but by then my manager, John, had heard. His eldest son, who works for him at his company, Champions, had called him, saying, 'Dad, it's all over Sky News – Bill's been arrested.'

'Has he rung the office?'

'No.'

'He hasn't called me?!'

John couldn't understand it, because he knew that he was the only person I *would* call.

At the time he was on a train from Loughborough to London for a meeting with some of the senior people at *The Telegraph* newspaper – which was probably the last place he wanted to be as the story was breaking.

Then, as he was walking into the boardroom, a call came from a sergeant at Leyland police station to say they had me there.

I came on the line and told him what had happened.

He said, 'Don't worry, Bill. But tell me, what have they done?'

'They've read out the charges and given me a duty lawyer.'

'Then the first thing you do is sack him.'

When the police had first said to me, 'Do you want a lawyer?' I'd actually replied, 'No, I don't think so.' I mean, I was that naïve about it.

John arranged for a lawyer he knew to come up to Leyland as soon as possible. It was going to take about three hours for him to get there, so I sat in a prison cell all that time, which felt like an eternity.

When eventually he did arrive, the police questioned me. Interestingly, one of the policemen said to him, 'Don't worry, I don't think Mr Roache is going to be charged.'

That was because they had to send the details to the Crown Prosecution Service and wait for their reply, and they were absolutely convinced it wouldn't happen. But then the CPS did charge me. And it just went on from there.

***

I trusted John completely. And he was to be a big part of everything that happened in the months to come.

I'd met him years before he became my manager. He and his company represent many celebrities and run big sporting events for charity, so it wasn't surprising that we first met at a charity dinner. John's sister, Jane, had been born with learning disabilities, and the dinner was to raise money for Rainbows, a children's hospice based in Loughborough, near John's office. Through John's connection with Rainbows, I've continued to support this brilliant charity ever since. John and I became good friends, and later, in around 2000, he became my manager.

The thing was, in the wake of the horrendous situation with Jimmy Savile, John had told me I might be a target, because at that time celebrities were being accused of similar crimes. I really hadn't thought any more about it, but he later told me he'd been concerned for a lot of the public figures he represented, and he'd prepared the team at Champions.

John's theory was that two significant media interviews I'd done had some part to play in my arrest: my Piers Morgan interview in 2012, and my more recent interview with New Zealand journalist Garth Bray, which had stirred up all the press furore before and during that New Zealand trip.

Piers Morgan's Life Stories aired on 13 April 2012. It was an hour-long interview on primetime ITV. The interview series had been running for some time – this was series 7 – and Piers had had many well-known figures talk to him, from Frank Bruno to James Corden. At that time he was the editor of the *Daily Mirror* – the youngest editor in the newspaper's history – and a celebrity in his own right.

Ken's colourful relationship history on the Street was Piers' way into talking about my personal life. Ken's had 22 girlfriends, four wives (if you count both marriages to Deirdre), three children – Susan, Peter and Daniel – and a step-daughter, Tracey. In my real life, it's been no secret that my first marriage failed because I'd been unfaithful. I was working away from home five nights a week and the opportunity to stray was there. I deeply regret this, and because of it I lost my marriage and was separated from my two older children, Linus and Vanya, for some time. But I certainly wasn't Ken, going from one marriage to the next. In my marriage to Sara I had been completely faithful, and we had been together for 31 years and had three beautiful children, Verity, Edwina and William.

Nevertheless, Piers persisted in asking me how many women I'd slept with and I said I did not know. He started throwing numbers around. This was personal, and I didn't want to talk about it. So I deflected his questions with a shrug or a 'maybe', and at one stage I even jokingly pretended to walk off-stage to show I didn't really appreciate his line of questioning. When he continued to press me for numbers and asked if it was 1,000 women, all I said was: 'It could be. I don't know.'

Well, it went viral – 'Bill Roache slept with 1,000 women.' For the next day or so it became the biggest Twitter story in the world. And I'd never said I had, but I took it with good humour. Piers' angle, I think, was that Ken – and I – were more active and interesting than had been claimed by his rival newspaper, *The Sun*, back in 1991, which had led to my libel action against them.

At the time I had no idea that this interview was creating an impression of me that was entirely wrong. Looking back, it seems that it was certainly a trigger for the later claims, however unintentional.

The interview with Garth Bray for New Zealand Television took place on 19 March 2013, before I was to fly to New Zealand to do the *Coronation Street* play. *Coronation Street* is very popular in New Zealand (they call it 'Coro' over there), which is why we were about to tour the play in Auckland, Wellington, Nelson and Christchurch.

Garth came to see me on set on the Street, and we chatted on the cobbles and in an indoor studio. I was about to learn a huge lesson from that interview and the media uproar that followed.

In the interview, I tried to explain reincarnation, but I should have known better. Reincarnation is a very complex subject, and unless the people you are talking to have an understanding of it, there's no point in trying to talk about it. You can't explain it in five minutes and answer controversial questions in soundbites, and I shouldn't have tried to. I blame myself for that. The press did misquote me, but not intentionally. If that situation were to come up again, I would say, 'Look, I'm not going to attempt to explain it to you. If you wish to know about it, go and study the Buddhist teachings on it, because they're as close to my views as anything I know.'

But at the time, the media really hounded me, and all I could do was issue a huge apology to anyone who had been upset by my comments. I hadn't intended to cause anyone any offence or distress. And I didn't feel any anger towards Garth or the other journalists involved. It was my fault for trying to answer their questions in the first place. Unfortunately, though, it added to the misleading impression being given of me.

**

When I got home from Leyland police station, shocked and exhausted, the media were again totally blocking my gate and the road outside the house. Fortunately I managed to get in, and was so happy and relieved to find my family there waiting for me. John had called them, and Verity and Will had managed to get out of the flat they shared in London with the help of Paddy, Verity's

In my army uniform,
when I'd just been
commissioned, 1953

Age 28, when I started on
Coronation Street, 1960

Raising awareness for motorcycle safety through wearing
a helmet. I'm pictured here on my own bike, 1976

Interpreting an astrology chart for a *Coronation Street* colleague, 1977

Opening a fair in Ely, Cambridgeshire, 1978

Taking time out on the *Coronation Street* set with Annie and Christabel Finch, who played Annie's screen daughter, Tracy, at the time, 1979

With Tony Warren, creator of *Coronation Street*, and Harry Kershaw, writer and long-term producer, 1990

Sara and I on our wedding day, 1978

Edwina's christening, with (L to R) Eileen Derbyshire,
Verity, Edwina, Betty Driver and Sara, 1984

Family portrait with Sara, Verity and newborn Will, 1986

Family portrait, 1990. Back row L to R: my nephew, Christopher; Christopher's wife, Jenny; Linus; Linus's wife, Ros; me; Verity; my father-in-law, Sid. Front row L to R: my niece, Jane; my sister, Beryl; my mother; Sara; Will; my mother-in-law, Kay.

On the fairway at
Rossendale Golf
Club, 1984

Enjoying a round of
golf with Gary Player
at Turnberry, 1988

At home with Will, Verity and Sara, looking after the litter
of nine puppies produced by our Labrador, Ella, 1989

With my mother at the
gates of Rutland House,
Ilkeston, Derbyshire,
where I grew up, 1993

My screen wife, Annie (left), and my real wife, Sara (right),
at the *Coronation Street* annual birthday party, 1995

Meeting the
Queen during her
visit to Preston,
Lancashire, 2002

With Linus in the Rovers for the *Coronation Street* fiftieth anniversary, 2010

Surprise! The moment when my family burst out of the Rovers on my 80th birthday, 2012. L to R: Will, Ros, Linus, Toby, Vanya, me, Verity.

Receiving an Honorary Doctor of Letters Degree
from the University of Chester, 2007

With Sinitta at the annual celebrity charity ball,
The Dorchester Hotel, 2017

Speaking at the Champions annual ball for
Rainbows Children's Hospice, 2015

On stage with my manager, John Hayes, 2016

The Farmfoods British Par 3 Golf Championship
at Nailcote Hall, Warwickshire, 2016

All images courtesy of William Roache unless otherwise stated.

boyfriend, who had dropped everything and driven them up to Manchester and away from all the press camped on their doorstep.

The press stayed outside my gate for about a week and I didn't go out to speak to them; I didn't want to speak to anybody. I just stayed at home with my family.

Then we found that the trial wasn't going to be for nearly a year, and of course Granada had to suspend me, but they still supported me right through the case. They were wonderful. I had nothing but complete support from them and from my family. Will and Verity quickly decided to move back in for the year, Linus came over from New York and I was in regular email contact with Vanya, who was living with her partner in Chichester.

I had nothing but support from my colleagues and friends, too. Several of my *Coronation Street* co-stars were to be character witnesses for me when the time came: Annie Kirkbride, Helen Worth (Gail McIntyre) and Chris Gascoyne (my on-screen son Peter). I have a great relationship with Chris, and he, like my other friends on the Street, was so supportive.

Ken Cope, a wonderful actor from the early days of *Coronation Street*, also very kindly offered to be a character witness (and true to form was very funny), as did Lucy Tucker, whom I had met as a young girl.

If you believe in someone, you support them no matter what. That's what true friends are about, and that's what John did for me, and continues to do. He's always so positive and forward-thinking. He does whatever needs to be done, and whatever is right, and I will never stop appreciating his friendship and loyalty, and indeed the support of the whole Hayes family.

They say celebrities are no different from other people, and we're not. But what is different is that whenever anything happens to us, it's in the media. And once it's out there, in a total reversal of the normal procedure, we're guilty until proven innocent. So I couldn't really go out, but I didn't want to. I didn't want to meet anybody. I became something of a recluse, but I did venture out to a restaurant once or twice during that year, and people said, 'Good on you,' and 'Don't worry.' I didn't hear one single negative comment or remark from anyone about the whole thing.

For the most part, I just stayed at home and I meditated a lot. What I always do when faced with a serious problem is look at the situation and take myself into the worst possible scenario. So I did that, thinking: *This is the law, things can happen, things that you don't think will happen can happen...* Having looked at that scenario, I accepted that it was a possibility.

Then I stepped back and thought, *No, I'm now going to be very positive and very optimistic, and look forward to the time out that I've got with my family, with no commitments at all.* And I stood in my own harmlessness. I know I'm a very gentle person. I can't bear to upset anybody in any way at all, and I go out of my way to avoid that happening. So I stood in that, stood in all those things, and took an optimistic view. And I felt okay.

From then on, it only took about three weeks, with the help of meditation, to get into feeling positive. It happened relatively quickly.

If a difficult situation comes to you, you must accept it. Don't be, 'Oh, why me? I'm a victim.' No! You certainly mustn't let fear come in or feel like a victim in any way at all, because you're not; we're not. Life will test us at certain times, but those tests are there to help us to get to know ourselves, to strengthen ourselves and grow. Challenges wake us up, get us thinking and open our mind.

So, when life does throw things at you, you must look at them, accept them, even embrace them. What I do is examine my response to the situation. There may be something in my thinking or my attitude, perhaps not directly connected with what's happening, that could be a bit better, so I always look at how I can improve myself. And we can become stronger and wiser as a result of challenges.

However, life never gives us more than we can deal with. I knew that. Also, everything passes. I knew that, too. So I knew I would get through this. And, as I reflected, *There are people worse off than me in the world – far worse off. There are people living in terrible conditions, people with war raging around them, people with terminal illnesses.*

My health remained really good and I also felt my consciousness was somehow raised during that year at home, because I became really aware of life and of its purpose. What I already understood about the universe and humanity was confirmed: we are loving, forgiving beings. And we need to rise above things to see the bigger picture – to understand the eternal nature of our existence.

Of course, I missed work. I was out of the Street for around 14 months in all, but in a way it was the first time in however many years – 54 or so – that I didn't have a script to learn or something to do. There were no personal appearances, no interviews and no work. And I must say I quite enjoyed that.

Looking back, I could see that year out as a gift. I was never alone and I had more time with my family than ever before. It was obviously a very frightening time for them, but they were wonderful – so loving and supportive. They virtually gave up their careers during that time. Will, like Linus, is also an actor, and Verity is a Reiki healer and interior designer.

She described it to me later: 'Daddy, you know at the very beginning I had a kind of vision – you know, like when you go into an aquarium and you have all the fish over the top of you in a sort of dome? Well, we were walking through a tunnel like that and it was a completely lovely space. The world was happening outside, away from us. It was like that, wasn't it?'

It was. That was how we coped. We created a sanctuary.

We played endless games. Linus and I invented a kind of triathlon of golf, chess and backgammon that we called 'The White Cottage Cup' after the name of our house. The garden here isn't big – it just wraps around the house, half an acre or so, but there's room for pitching and putting. Sometimes we'd still be playing when it was getting dark and Will would be calling us in and we'd say, 'Ah, yes, just a bit longer… Got to finish this round!'

We watched comedy a lot, too, for some distraction – Will and Verity love *Gavin and Stacey* and the film *Blades of Glory*, and we spent many nights just watching those and other comedy films and series to lift our spirits. Whatever's happening in your life, you don't need to feel bad about feeling okay for a little while. And humour is a great healer.

Because of that and my daily meditation, I didn't get upset or depressed. I was taking a positive view of the outcome.

I know it was pretty difficult for my children, but we talked a lot and didn't keep anything back. It was the same when they lost their mother. That was terrible, such a shock, but we all kept talking, and if one of us was at a low ebb, the others would get right in there so nobody felt alone or tearful for too long. Will and Verity are also brilliant at doing that for each other – they are good friends as well as siblings. We've always been very close, so I can't say the court case year brought us closer, but it reminded us of the closeness that was already there.

***

The trial drew nearer until finally the first day, 14 January 2014, arrived.

A lovely man, security officer Steve Spencer, who also worked for Granada, came to take us to Preston Crown Court. The media again were at the gate. Steve was a tower of strength, seeing us to the court, seeing us out and generally looking after us every day of the trial. He was wonderful, and very intelligent too – we would talk about how the case was progressing in the car on the way there and back, and we'd go over it together. And John Hayes and his wife, Donna, moved to Preston for the duration of the trial so he could be with me in court every day. He was a very busy man, and he took nearly a month out. I really appreciated that he and his wife were there for me, and they both gave me amazing support. They were brilliant.

And, pretty much, the trial itself just went through its process.

It took three and a half weeks, and the one day that I was slightly nervous was the day I was going to be in the witness box. I wanted to make sure I was alert and that I heard everything. And of course I just wanted to speak the truth. It must be terrible if you're covering up something and you're lying in the witness box, because you've got to remember your lines. I spoke the truth and just hoped that it would all come out okay.

John thought that the jury could be out for a few days, but they came back in under three hours with unanimous verdicts. When they were being read out, I didn't actually hear the 'not' on some of them, just the 'guilty'. But I saw that Steve was clapping and Verity was crying. Then I realized that all was well.

And that was that. It was all over. It was time to get back to work.

***

As I said at the time, in that situation there were no winners. I don't feel any resentment. We have to be forgiving, because, as I explained earlier, forgiving releases us.

It's not easy talking about hard times, but it's good to talk, because I believe in learning from what happens to us and going forwards. We have to go forwards in life and do what needs to be done. We just have to deal with it.

SUMMARY: SURVIVING TOUGH TIMES

- First of all, face what's happening; be realistic about it and don't try to put your head under the covers. Have a good look at it.

- Clear out anything within yourself that in any way could be part of it, no matter how small it might be, maybe a thought or an attitude. Clear that out of the way.

- Accept fully anything that's coming at you, and know that however helpless you may feel, life will not throw something at you that you cannot deal with. Life is always trying to help you. If something comes at you, it's to strengthen you, help you to get rid of any negativity within and enable you to move forwards as a positive being. The tougher it is, the stronger you're going to be when you've overcome it.

- How do you overcome it? Just ask for help. People don't ask the universe for help enough. Those around us – angel and guides – want to help, but because of our free will, they cannot do so unless we ask. So ask the universe, ask the angels, ask whatever or whoever you think is around you; just ask for help.

- Also, know that this will pass. In the end, all will be well, and if it isn't well, it isn't the end. To be in the human condition isn't easy, but once you take a wider view and open up to your eternal state, your true spiritual self, life is much easier, because you see the bigger, eternal picture. You know that all things must pass. And life is always moving upwards and onwards.

Chapter 5

LIFELONG WELLBEING

First of all, I have to say I'm not an expert, telling you what to do, I'm just saying what works for me. Through meditation and trusting my knowing, I've come closer and closer to being my true self, who I really am, and who we all are, at heart – peaceful, loving human beings who are connected to one another and to everything around us. Understanding this and being at peace with ourselves – fully accepting, loving and forgiving ourselves – means it's so much easier to care for ourselves – eating well and being fit and healthy, but really enjoying life, too. I feel good. And I hope what I share in this chapter will help you to feel good, too.

I've never gone in for extreme diets or exercise. I don't have a regime; I just take a balanced, common-sense approach and try to keep my sense of humour. People who throw themselves into exercise or extreme diets may be missing out – because if we focus intensely on one thing, we're neglecting something else. We won't be in balance, and when this happens, we tend to lose that bigger, grander, calmer, more peaceful and absolutely beautiful sense of wholeness that is ours to enjoy.

Everything is one, and it's understanding this that's important – way more so than which brand of gluten-free organic rye bread to eat. When we're not in balance, and not feeling that oneness, it can lead to stress, upset and illness.

So a little bit of eating the wrong things and not exercising is okay – we don't have to feel that we have to get up at 6 a.m. for a run then eat cabbage leaves all day! We do have to enjoy life, though, to enjoy what we do, and if we don't enjoy doing something, we don't need to do it. So before I tell you what works for me in terms of caring for ourselves, let's throw 'shoulds' and 'oughts' out of the window.

Beliefs

Before we look at the practical steps to wellbeing, we need to look at beliefs. Take ageing, for an example. Ageing is a belief system within the collective consciousness of humanity. It's what we've collectively decided about age and what it means for our body and our lifestyle.

First of all, there's a general belief in our society that when you retire, you're redundant. This is totally wrong. The Native Americans did the right thing: as they became older, they became the wise ones who taught the children. While the parents were busy hunting and sorting things out, the children were taught by the elders, who were highly respected. They had a role; they weren't thought of as redundant.

Being considered redundant as we age shouldn't be acceptable. It's casting aside the wisdom that people – all kinds of people – have acquired through their lifetimes. We should benefit from this rather than reject it.

Aside from the contribution that can be made by older people, there are certain personal benefits to ageing. There are fewer demands upon you in later life, which gives you greater freedom. Your sensitivity and intuition are more honed and you can rely on them more, as you're less distracted by hurt and upset. You become more relaxed, more aware and a little wiser, and get closer to your true, eternal self.

> Think of ageing not only as growing in knowledge, but also as growing in self-knowledge and wisdom.

Often, ageing is thought of as physical decline, but we can still stay balanced and healthy and enjoy life as we age. The body renews its cells all the time: every seven years we're made up of a completely new set of cells. If we have the attitude of 'I'm getting older, therefore I'm getting weaker,' our energy drops, and our cells renew at a lower rate. To counter this, we can decide to say, 'No, I'm not having this,' and instead think that every time our cells renew themselves, they're going to be newer, younger, healthier, rejuvenated cells. Then we will get younger, healthier and more rejuvenated and beautiful all the time. Through this thought, we will increase our lifespan and improve our health.

Each morning as I come out of the shower, I say, 'Every cell renews itself as a younger, healthier and rejuvenated cell, therefore I am getting younger, healthier and I am rejuvenating.' So I've got a little morning ritual there, but I say it whenever it comes to mind as well. It can't hurt, can it?!

You are what you think. That's a cliché, but it's true. The way you think is going to give you the life you get. If you're pessimistic and always looking for trouble, you'll find trouble. If you're optimistic and believe everything is beautiful and wonderful, beautiful and wonderful things are more likely to happen to you. There will still be the other human things happening, but to a large extent how you think is going to dictate how you live, and certainly your ageing process.

If I ever have an ailment, for example, I think of myself as being in perfect health. I know this can help the body to heal. This type of thinking is what's known as the Law of Attraction – like attracts like. What we think about most manifests in our life, so what we focus on can actually create our reality. In a nutshell, thoughts manifest reality.

I do try to look after myself – to think positively, give myself calm time and live in balance and harmony with myself and my surroundings – and I'm sure that has benefited my health. I've barely had a serious illness in my life. As I mentioned earlier, I once had a small duodenal ulcer that burst, and I lost four pints of blood because it had gone straight onto an artery, but that was soon healed, and I've had no problems since. My hearing has not been good, but that's nothing to do with age. It's the result of an accident when I was 21 and in the army. I was on a three-inch mortar training course in Chiseldon, Wiltshire, when a bomb detonated close to where I was standing, which left me totally deaf for around three weeks. I lost 50 per cent of my hearing, but I've learned to live with it.

When I was coming up to my 80th birthday and was on tour in Canada for *Coronation Street*, I did have a really bad cold, so I was dosed up with medicine, and instead of going out and sightseeing I stayed in bed every day and just got up to do the performance in the evening. I did manage to get out to see Niagara Falls, and I'm glad I did that, but by the time we hit our last city on the tour I'd decided to see a doctor, because I really wasn't getting any better. He said, 'You've got pneumonia.'

Well, I was due to fly home shortly anyway, so I carried on, and as soon as I got back I went to my own doctor, who confirmed the diagnosis. I got antibiotics and soon recovered. The fact that I thought I only had a bad cold probably helped!

When you think positively and know that deteriorating with age is a belief system, you begin to see that any ailments you have don't have to be part of the ageing process. And you do something about them. If you've got a pain, there's a reason for that; you deal with it. You'd get an ailment seen to in your twenties or thirties, so why not in later life? Don't ever think, *Oh, that's age*, and accept it. Give yourself the attention and care you deserve to deal with the problem on the physical level.

When my eyesight began to deteriorate, I went to an optician, who said, 'How old are you?' I replied, 'Forty-five,' and he said, 'That's what it is.' I decided it wasn't that. And I got a book, *Better Eyesight without Glasses*, by a Dr Bates, and started exercising my eye muscles as it suggested. I could feel those muscles working, and I delayed my need for glasses by 12–15 years.

Also, we don't have to age and die at a certain time. We can extend our lifespan by pushing the parameters of the belief that we'll only live to 70, 80 or 90 years. Many people are now living for 100 years or more, and this can change our reality. If it continues, more and more people will start living to be 100, 120, 130, 140. It can happen. After all, the human body was originally designed to last for as long as we wanted it to before we decided to go back to our true home. So we can push the parameters of ageing for ourselves, and when we do this, we contribute to the collective consciousness of humanity. By pushing society's assumptions about lifespan, we'll move it on. Then others will push it on further, and the collective consciousness will move on further. Eventually we'll live to be 200 years or more.

On my 84th birthday I said, 'I'm going to get younger every year.' It was a joke, but there was a kind of truth behind it. And that's how I feel.

Taking Care of Yourself

Realizing you don't have to decline with age doesn't mean you can drink a bottle of whisky or have a cheeseburger every day. You still have the responsibility of taking care of your body. But the rules, in my view, are very simple.

Smoking

We often make life choices out of habit rather than through thinking about them. If you smoke, for example, you have made a choice to damage your health and shorten your life. Never kid yourself – smoking kills you. It causes cancer, it causes emphysema and it causes a whole lot of other illnesses. There's no question about that. I saw this first hand with Annie Kirkbride. Smoking is really, really bad for your health.

I say this as someone who smoked about 40 a day up to the age of 40. To give it up, I made myself watch films about lung cancer and all the other horrible smoking-related diseases I didn't want to face. I made myself read up on what smoking did, the actual effects it had on the body, and I took it all in.

I didn't want to use aids for stopping smoking, because I didn't want to get dependent on patches or gum or whatever else was out there at the time. It would have been a crutch and it wasn't right for me. I just built up a picture whereby I knew that every puff I took was harming my health and shortening my life. If you need to give up, you can build that picture, too. You can think of smoking as inhaling a poison – a slow, gentle poison that is going to make you ill one way or another. Don't shy away from the facts of what smoking does to you. Look at them.

After a time I got to a point where I began to question myself: 'What am I doing? I am smoking because I want to, when I know it's killing me.' I'd got those two warring factions – the desire to smoke and the knowledge of how awful it was – on a pretty even pegging. You have to do this. If you want to give up and say to yourself, 'Stop it, don't do it,' when part of you is still saying, 'But I like smoking,' you're fighting a losing battle.

It was getting near Christmas and I decided that I would smoke as much as I wanted up to New Year's Eve and then I'd give up. And I made myself smoke almost more than I wanted – I suppose I was building up a kind of aversion. On New Year's Eve I had about five cigarettes left in a packet. I threw them on the fire and thought, *That's that*, and I was actually relieved. I said to myself, 'If I can't stop doing something that I know is killing me, then I can't do anything. I'm useless as a human being.'

In the year or so afterwards, if I ever felt tempted to smoke, I never gave in, because I thought of what smoking did to you, and that gave me the strength to give up and never smoke again. Now that may not work for everybody, but it did it for me. The desire to smoke subsided with time, and now I have no desire to smoke at all.

I know giving up isn't an easy thing to do and I have tremendous sympathy for anyone going through it. I'd had earlier, failed attempts at giving up. Before I built up that picture of how ill smoking makes you, I'd convince myself I could have just one cigarette, for example after a meal when people were passing them around. But sure enough, the smoking would get going again. From experience, I know that you can't just have one cigarette. You can't – you're an addict. But in time you can recover.

Sleep

If you wake up in the morning feeling tired, there's something not right. The body repairs itself during sleep, so if you're missing out on sleep, you're missing out on healing. You might need to adjust your bedtime to harmonize with the sleep pattern your body naturally needs.

Although there's a tendency to need less sleep as you get older, I sleep for around eight hours a night. I go to bed at 11 or 12 p.m. and get up between 7 and 8 a.m., whether I'm working or not. This routine helps my body get the rest it needs, and when I wake up, I feel rejuvenated. And I make sure I'm calm before bed. I go into the quiet, as I call it, into the silence, to prepare for sleep, so I'm relaxed and sleep well.

Alcohol

I drank for England in the 1960s. I just thought it was normal to come home and have a couple of gin and tonics, half a bottle of wine with dinner and maybe a brandy afterwards, and that was every day. I have just the odd glass now on special occasions, but that's me. Find a balance that's right for you. Again, everything in moderation.

Water

We're about 65 per cent water, and generally we don't drink enough of it. It's all very well getting it in sugary, fizzy drinks or in tea or coffee, but we need to drink fresh water, too. If you aren't doing so, just try drinking a glass a day to start off with. Pure water is a beautiful drink. See it as a life-giving elixir.

Exercise

Exercise is widely promoted, but in my experience you don't have to pound the pavements every morning going for a jog or keep going to the gym. I'm healthy and reasonably fit without that. I work full time, and I have the energy for everything I need to do – filming, meetings and publicity work. Sometimes we'll be filming for up to 12 hours a day if there's a heavy storyline. I might be in four or five scenes a day, then get home and need to learn or brush up on lines for the next day. Acting itself can be very physical, and the challenge of it, with new storylines coming in, gives me energy and keeps me sharp.

The main thing here is that whatever form of exercise you do, you enjoy it. If you don't enjoy it and it feels like punishment, don't do it! Find an activity that makes you feel good while you're doing it, rather than only good when you stop!

Taking brisk walks is a good thing, and I do prioritize getting fresh air. I recently took up golf again, which I play very regularly. Every Thursday and Saturday I also attend a one-hour 'fun fit' session where we're really put through our paces – running, walking, basketball, boxing – it gets the heart rate up and raises a sweat.

Posture

Posture is really important. As an actor, the first thing you do if you want to age is put your head forwards. Of course, you don't want to do that, so try to stay upright. If you can keep your posture right, everything will flow. Imagine your body being like a hosepipe – if you bend it, it stops the flow of water. If you're walking round like that, it can't help your circulation, as everything that needs to flow won't be flowing.

So, especially when you stand, just be aware of your posture. I'm lucky, because my children are always saying, 'Put your shoulders back, Daddy, come on.' It's good to have family that nag at you a bit. I call Verity and Will my 'irritants'.

Every so often I'll lie on the floor on my back for 10 minutes or so to straighten my spine and try to feel my own alignment – where my head is naturally most comfortable – and take that feeling with me when I stand up.

Like everything else I'm sharing with you, though, this doesn't mean you have to go to extremes. There's no need to be overly rigid and upright. But when I'm walking, I become aware of how I'm holding my body, and I know it's better if I stand tall, because I walk more briskly and easily.

Also, I try not to be sedentary. If I'm at work at the studios in Manchester, I'll often take a stroll around the set between scenes. I drive myself to work, so I try to keep myself moving as much as I can during the day – and I do stand up a lot rather than sit, which helps my posture and circulation. At home, I'll watch some television with my arm against the mantelpiece, or, if I'm watching television in the kitchen, I'll stand and lean against a unit. I told my doctor this, and when I went to see him a few weeks later, he'd had his desk raised and was seeing patients standing up!

Natural Self-Help

Doctors can be invaluable, but we needn't go running to them for prescriptions for every little thing – we can help ourselves in so many ways. I opt for homoeopathic remedies, natural products and relaxation techniques rather than reach for a painkiller. I take *Nux vomica* to help digestion, for example, and when I started getting dry, itchy skin on my lower legs, I just applied coconut oil morning and evening, which stopped it. I also use it to keep my face moisturized. But I will use allopathic medicines when I think they're necessary.

Sometimes a simple remedy does work just as well, though. When I started getting dry, itchy eyes, I was given ointments and all sorts of eye drops with chemicals in them, but I found that simple salt and water did the trick.

Salt Water for Dry Eyes

- *I boil some water and pour it into a blue bottle (the blue pigment reduces the amount of light reaching the water, which is believed to help preserve it).*

- *I then have Himalayan salt, some cottonwool buds and two egg cups ready. I pour some of the boiled water into one egg cup (about 1 cm/half an inch deep), add* about two pinches of the salt and mix it with one of the cotton buds until fully dissolved.

- With one eye closed, I wipe the corner of my eye with the cotton bud, then wipe right across, then wipe the other corner, leaving quite a bit of salt water on it (sometimes it stings a bit, but that's okay).

- I throw that cotton bud away, then repeat for the other eye.

I do this every morning and every night, and whenever I feel my eyes are getting dry. It works! If you don't have any Himalayan salt, you can use rock salt, but not the refined domestic salt.

If I get back pain, I do this:

BREATHING THROUGH BACK PAIN

- Standing, lean back on your heels as far as you comfortably can without losing your balance, so your back is absolutely straight.

- *Then imagine that you're breathing in from your heels and taking your breath from your heels through your spine right to the top of your head.*

- *Then breathe out through your spine.*

This can bring instant relief and allows healing to take place.

Food That Nourishes

I was lucky, growing up. It was during the war years, when food was quite scarce and we were told to eat every little bit of it. And we had an allotment. My mother used to take me off there and we'd grow lots of vegetables. I remember eating tomatoes – they used to taste so wonderful. There were barely any sweets at all then, which meant I sometimes used to fantasize about them, but I do feel for some of the children I see walking around today with a cola in one hand and a bar of chocolate in the other. I can't help thinking, *Oh my God, that's loaded with sugar – what hope have they got?* I know their taste buds will become accustomed to that sort of thing and it will be really tough on them to try anything different. When you're young, your body tends to cope with what you throw at it, but it's only coping; if you're not eating well, you're not really looking after yourself.

If you go into a supermarket today and look along the shelves, you'll see that most of the foods contain chemicals, preservatives and colourings that are not good for us. You'll have to go the organic section to be sure that there are no impurities in the products on display.

My approach is to eat as much natural food as possible – nature provides everything we need. I have butter, as fat-free spreads can be full of chemicals. And I drink full-cream milk, because skimmed and semi-skimmed milk can have the goodness taken out of them. My preferences now are almond milk and goats' butter. Most things labelled 'fat-free' will have chemical additives.

I also eat as many fresh vegetables as I comfortably can. My breakfast every morning is a shake of three vegetables, including celery and carrots, one fruit, maybe blueberries, some protein mix, a little turmeric and apple cider vinegar or coconut oil. Will got me into shakes, and now they're a habit. They're much easier to make than a cooked breakfast, and I'm getting most of my vegetables and lots of other goodies in first thing. I'm not saying I'm perfect for the rest of the day, but I'm lucky that at Granada they have a huge salad bar, so I'll have a plateful of salad for lunch with meat or fish.

I keep my evening meal basic – no pre-prepared ready-meals. I know it's tempting to have them when you live on your own! Luckily, I like many foods that are naturally good. There was a time when they said eggs were bad for you, but eggs are a most wonderful cocktail of vitamins. One Italian woman, Emma Morano, had two raw eggs every day, and she lived until she was 117. I have eggs pretty well every day as well, because I like them. Enjoyment is key when it comes to eating. You can eat in a balanced way, bringing natural foods into your diet, and enjoy it too. It doesn't have to be difficult.

I do watch my sugar intake. I don't eat much fruit, because it's usually high in sugar, and I look at the list of ingredients on any foods I buy. If a label says carbohydrates of which sugars are more than 10g per 100g, that item is not good for you. And if you look at the so-called healthy breakfast cereals – the mueslis – some of them are actually 40 per cent sugar or more. So watch the sugar – be sensible about it. You can have a bit of chocolate in the evening if you want to, but instead of hogging a whole box (like I used to!), just have a bit now and then. I do this – I'm not going to deny myself! Go for the darker varieties, though – those with around

70 per cent cocoa or more. Dark chocolate contains less sugar, is full of good minerals, can be good for the heart and circulation, and of course gives you a little endorphin boost.

I learned about the dangers of sugar just before I was 80, when I had my annual blood test. I have a very good doctor, Dr Amar Ahmed, who looks after me very well, and after my blood test he said, 'I'm sorry to tell you, Bill, but you're Type 2 diabetic.'

And I looked at him in disbelief and said, 'I'm not!'

I went to see the nurse and we went through my diet. My sugar intake was horrendous. Nearly everything I was buying was 20g, 30g, 50g sugar per 100g – way over the healthy amount. On top of that I had honey in tea, and if I drove to London I'd buy chocolate bars, pop them on the passenger seat and munch my way to the capital. Every meal after dinner I would prowl the house for chocolate! I'm amazed I got to 80 without anything worse happening.

So I just cut out all of it – if any product had more than 10g of sugar per 100g, I didn't buy it. That was difficult. But after five weeks – and that's all it was – *whoomph*, the sugar cravings went. I didn't want chocolate any more, I lost a few pounds in weight, my energy levels became constant and I felt good.

So I went back to Dr Ahmed and said, 'Look, all is well. I've cut the sugar out and I'm not Type 2 diabetic any more.'

He said, 'Well, you are really, you know, because if you were to go back...'

I said, 'If I were to go back, I'd be poisoning myself. It's just that I ate too much sugar.'

Around the same time, my manager had taken out a life insurance policy for me (not easy to get when you're 80). And when Dr Ahmed had sent the insurance company my medical report listing Type 2 diabetes, they'd come back offering just half the potential payout I would have received if I hadn't been diagnosed as diabetic.

So I said to John, 'Forget it. I'm not Type 2 diabetic, and I'm certainly not having that insurance policy.'

But then the insurance company said, 'Okay, we'll do a surprise blood test on you,' which they did. It was perfectly all right and they offered the full amount of insurance.

So that's how I found out I was eating too much sugar. I learned that we don't need much and we can get it all from fruit. We might worry about our fat and salt intake – and again, we need everything in moderation – but the real enemy of our wellbeing is too much sugar. That was a big awakening for me.

Since I've cut my sugar intake, I've been able to maintain a lighter weight, around 11 stone 8 pounds, which feels healthy for me. My energy is more consistent throughout the day, too – I no longer suffer from blood-sugar lows – and my sweet tooth is under control. Well, most of the time!

If I feel hungry between meals, I drink some water. It does work, so try it before you resort to a snack. Remember that as your body feels the need for food, it starts to absorb fat to convert into energy. So feeling hungry means you are losing fat. Make a positive out of feeling hungry, and the hunger feeling soon wears off. I'm not saying do this all the time – you may need a small snack on occasion, we all do – but drinking water also gives you time to be really aware of the hunger and think, *Do I really need food or is this just a habit?* rather than diving straight into the fridge. However, I know how difficult it is when you feel hungry, so I always have some nuts around.

Bread is my weakness. I love it. Toast is so friendly, and afternoon tea – with sandwiches – used to be my favourite meal. When I first started to reduce my sugar intake, I didn't realize that bread, as a carbohydrate, makes sugar (yes, I know it seems obvious now, but I really didn't know it at the time). I was cutting out sugary foods, but eating bread all day long until someone told me that. So you need to have an understanding of what you're putting into yourself and what it's doing to you. You don't have to cut out bread, but just be aware of how much you're eating, and moderate it. If you have a binge of carbohydrates one day, try to reduce them the next day. It's all about balance, harmony and common sense.

What also helps me is not bingeing on carbs in the evening. I'll often have a big salad with my main meal rather than a helping of rice, pasta or potato, which all just make me feel heavy and tired. I don't exercise after dinner – I no longer have our dog, Poppy, at home, as she now lives with Verity, so there's no evening dog-walking – so if I do eat lots of carbs at dinner time, I know I won't burn off those calories.

One of the best things about not eating lots of carbs at night, aside from not feeling stuffed, is that I have more energy the next day. I feel brighter and more awake in the mornings.

I don't cut out carbohydrates altogether, but I generally keep bread to one slice a day and find a way to enjoy a treat now and again. When I'm having afternoon tea with scones, for example, I'll have a little cream with them, but I won't have the jam. I'm aware that I'm taking in sugar and fat with the scones and cream, but I make sure I still enjoy them. What is life without the occasional treat?!

Sugar seems to deaden your palette, though, and when you cut it back, you're much more sensitive to what you're eating. When I eat now, I find there's so much flavour in the food, whereas before I'd often just be getting through a first course in anticipation of a sweet dessert. I remember having a mouthful of banana when I hadn't had sugar for weeks and it tasted so rich – almost like toffee – that I couldn't believe I'd wolfed down sugary cakes for so long without realizing the powerful effect sugar was having on my body.

Sugar can be so addictive. You have some, and then you want a bit more, and more again, as you get accustomed to it. I had years of sugar indulgence, but it's amazing how quickly, relatively speaking, the cravings disappeared. As I said earlier, I was free of them in a matter of weeks. And now I can taste everything – and everything tastes better.

The simplest meal can be really enjoyable. I remember walking around Paris and seeing one of the French guys in a market having his lunch. It was just a small plate of hot baby carrots with butter poured over them, and a bit of salt and pepper too, and it looked delicious. Just cooked carrots, but he knew how to enjoy them. And if you enjoy what you eat, it's much better for you. Just walk down that road as far as you can without making it difficult for yourself.

Simple Ways to Improve Your Diet

Here's how you might cut down on carbohydrates and sugar and make some dietary substitutions. I stress here that this is what works for me; you'll need to do what's right for you. The idea is to eat what you enjoy while keeping a careful eye on your sugar and carbohydrate intake.

Avoid: Sugary breakfast cereal
Try: Breakfast shake: three vegetables, one fruit

Avoid: Margarine or other processed spread
Try: Butter

Avoid: Skimmed milk
Try: Full-fat milk or almond milk

Avoid: Fizzy drinks
Try: Drinking more water

Avoid: Processed foods such as bacon, ham, ready-meals

Try: Keeping it simple: fish, a little meat (organic if possible), plenty of fresh vegetables

Avoid: Overdosing on bread

Try: One slice of bread a day

Avoid: Daily alcohol

Try: Alcohol in moderation: a glass of wine once a day maximum

Avoid: Treats every day: chocolate, cake, etc.

Try: A treat once or twice a week, in reduced quantity – but savour it! Try a little fruit as a substitute for sweet things.

Eating and Kindness

A mother once told me that when her son, who was four or five, was eating some meat, he asked where it came from. And she said, 'Well, it's a lamb.'

He said, 'A little lamb running around in the field?'

'Yes.'

'It's a wonder they don't bite us!'

Now that was a little child expressing his feelings. He was beginning to have an awareness that many of us have forgotten: that animals are killed for our benefit. We have blinkers on so much of the time that we don't see things the way they really are.

I don't like the killing of animals, so I was vegetarian for around about four or five years. I wasn't a strict one. If I was invited out for dinner and meat was served, I didn't think, *Ooh, I can't touch meat.* The hostess would have gone to a lot of trouble to make that meal, so I would eat it. For me, it was perfectly okay to do that.

I've now slipped a little from vegetarianism, because I found it difficult to get the protein. I'll eat chicken or other meat or fish occasionally, but I'll try not to eat any processed meat, and a lot of days won't eat any meat at all. I just try to be as natural and as simple as possible in life. We do tend to make it complicated!

If I do eat meat, I try to choose organic, as the animals tend to be better cared for. There are some individual farmers I know who are very kind in the way they raise their livestock. And I always thank the animal. The Native Americans understood the importance of this wonderfully; when they killed a buffalo, they would thank it and make sure they used every part of it. We need to be aware of the animals being killed for us, and how it is done. I know this may sound obvious, but the way we buy meat now can be so disconnected from the process of slaughter.

A recent item in the media demonstrated this point. People in a supermarket in Brazil were being offered cooked pieces of a new brand of pork sausage, and when one woman wanted to buy some, the guy pretended he'd run out. So he picked up a live piglet, opened the lid of a fake sausage machine right in front of her and put the piglet in. (What people didn't see was his assistant holding the piglet safe under the counter.) He closed the lid and cranked the handle as his able assistant secretly pushed out pre-made sausages. The customer cried out, 'Urgh!' and looked as though she wanted to be sick. Another woman hit him when he put the piglet in the machine, other people tried to open it to get the piglet out, and everyone was horrified – although they had all happily enjoyed the free sausage sample. It goes to show that when we're confronted with the reality of animal killing, we're horrified, and therefore are in denial.

It is our responsibility to make sure that animals are killed as humanely as possible, even lovingly dispatched. There should be no fear involved in the process, but I'm afraid it's far from perfect at the moment.

Do concern yourself with how animals are dealt with. Look into it a little bit; perhaps donate to charities seeking to make an improvement. You don't have to become vegetarian overnight, or an animal rights activist, but do make a little contribution if you can. And, if you eat meat, thank the animal for its gift to you. We need to understand and remember the sacrifice these animals have made.

As well as caring for animals, we need to care for the earth and the oceans – our soil is being ruined by chemical fertilizers and we're polluting the oceans, too. Think about this for a moment and try to understand the wholeness of our existence here. The animals, the earth and the oceans are made of the same energy as we are. If we harm them, or anything else, we harm ourselves, because we all share this one energy. It's in our own interest to care.

Also, if we start loving everything, then that love comes back to us. So we can do it for purely selfish reasons, but really, it is in our nature. So, love everything because you are a loving person, as we all are. If you're not being that loving person, you're not being true to yourself.

Relaxed Eating

There's a saying: 'If you eat in anger, you eat poison.' And that's absolutely true. If you're agitated or stressed when you eat, your stomach acid level goes up, your digestive system doesn't work properly and you don't get all the nutritional benefits from your food. This is why eating on the hoof or snatching a quick sandwich at your desk isn't good. If you're in a nice relaxed frame of mind, however, you will digest food beautifully and absorb it perfectly.

I know it's very difficult to be relaxed when eating in the society we live in. But before a meal I try to be as relaxed as I can. I don't necessarily eat slowly – if I chewed each mouthful 32 times, or whatever the latest recommendation is, I'd never get through a meal! But I try to enjoy what I eat. When we're relaxed, we enjoy our food, and we enjoy it all the more when it's wholesome food that our body will easily absorb.

Giving thanks or a blessing before a meal gives us a few moments to relax and slow down, so we digest our food well. You don't have to say the words out loud, you can just think them. When we do this, we also give ourselves a precious gift – we open up to being peaceful, loving and caring.

GIVING THANKS

The tradition of saying grace was originally a well-meaning one, but over time it went a bit awry, as religious rituals can do, and people just sort of quacked it out in a formulaic way. But really, no formula is needed, and it's a wonderful thing to thank the universe and the Earth for the food we are about to eat. There are many people in the world who don't have fresh food or water, so we're very, very fortunate, and it helps to appreciate that.

Before I eat, I go into a peaceful, calm state of being and give thanks for the food. If you would like to say your own grace, think of a simple statement. It doesn't need to be heavy. You might say:

> *Thank you for this wonderful food today.*
> *May more and more people have*
> *the food that they need.*

Overall, wellbeing is all about moderation and balance, as long as you know underneath (and don't kid yourself!)

what's good for you and what's not. If you're getting some exercise, drinking fresh water, getting the sleep you need, eating fresh vegetables and loving what's on your plate, fundamentally that's it. Nothing need be extreme.

Always go with what resonates with you. Never do anything that offends your reason, and try to *enjoy* everything. And if you follow this advice, you will naturally steer towards what is wholesome, caring, loving and best for you.

SUMMARY: THE BASICS OF A HEALTHY LIFE

- Don't go along with the myth that age inevitably brings decline. There's no need to just accept ailments for that reason; get them seen to and enjoy life.

- Think positively about your health. Your cells rejuvenate. Think positively about this renewal.

- If you smoke, plan how to give up – there is a lot of support available.

- Drink plenty of fresh water.

- Drink alcohol in moderation. The body is not designed to take alcohol.

- Walk every day. Get fresh air. Don't punish yourself with unachievable exercise regimes and diets.

- Check your posture.

- Go with natural remedies for minor ailments if you can.

- Make sure you get enough sleep, because the body heals itself during sleep.

- Avoid eating lots of processed foods containing additives. Keep your diet natural and wholesome.

- Eat as many fresh vegetables as you can each day.

- Watch your sugar and carbohydrate intake. Find a balance so you can have the odd treat. Always aim for balance and moderation in your diet.

- Care about animal welfare.

- Relax before you eat.

- Give thanks for the food you have.

- Enjoy your food!

- Always do what feels right for you. Go into your heart and ask for guidance from your true self if you need to. Listen to your intuition.

Chapter 6

INSPIRATIONAL PEOPLE

Many men and women are living longer, healthier lives. They may be in their late eighties or nineties; they may be centenarians (reaching 100 years plus) or supercentenarians (reaching 110 years and more). They have much to share on the secrets of long-term health and longevity.

What they share, above all, is a positive attitude: they're forward-looking and optimistic, often working towards goals and being part of something greater than themselves. This attitude is available to us all; just because some societies have decided ageing means automatic decline doesn't mean it is the truth. It is not the truth. Think differently about ageing, and you will live longer and contribute to a positive collective consciousness that will benefit everyone.

It takes only 4 per cent of the population to shift the collective consciousness. So if 4 per cent of the world's population – around 300,000,000 (300 million) people – expected to live a long, healthy and happy life, and affirmed this every day, this would become reality for all of us. Just a relatively small shift in our collective consciousness can have a big effect.

This was observed when researchers were studying macaque monkeys, a highly intelligent species native to Japan, on the island of Koshima. The monkeys liked sweet potatoes, but in an experiment the researchers covered the potatoes with a substance they didn't like, so none of them ate them. Then one monkey, Imo, started to wash the potatoes in the sea. Other monkeys in the troop soon followed suit. To the researchers' surprise, when a critical number of monkeys – just 4 per cent – had learned to wash the potatoes, monkeys on nearby islands adopted the same behaviour. They had never observed their fellow primates across the water washing the sweet potatoes, but the technique had been communicated through a shared, or group, consciousness.

When enough of us know how to truly live, we too will reach a tipping point – we'll create a shift in consciousness that will create happier, healthier and longer lives.

What Inspirational People Are Saying…

Centenarian doctor Shigeaki Hinohara is a wonderful example of just how much we can positively influence our health and lifespan. This award-winning Japanese physician, who lived until he was 105 and worked full time until he was 87, evidently didn't believe that ageing meant decline or lack of purpose. He wrote more than 150 books, including the million-copy bestseller *How to Live Well*, which was published in 2001, when he was 89. On top of this, he took up volunteering at 65.

His advice was simple. He recommended keeping active (taking the stairs rather than the lift, for example, and carrying your own belongings rather than letting others do it), maintaining a healthy weight and keeping a sense of purpose. He said, 'Keep working, keep learning and you will never get old.' He loved his own work in St Luke's Hospital and College in Tokyo, practising and teaching medicine. And his work ethic resonates with me, because I am one of those people who doesn't ever want to stop working, and believe it is always good to keep learning something new.

One of the great things that Dr Hinohara said was: 'Energy comes from feeling good, not from eating well or sleeping a lot.' Given I'm not the perfect role model when it comes to toast and cake, these words help to explain my own longevity. I do enjoy myself, and my work is really fulfilling. And that makes me feel better than following a strict diet or going to the gym.

If we enjoy something, then the universe enjoys it, too. In fact, the energy we give out when we're happy and enjoying something affects *everything*, not just in our universe, but in other universes and the whole cosmos. This is how a positive collective consciousness comes about; because we're all interconnected and part of the whole, we contribute whatever we're feeling to that whole. If we're negative, we're adding to the negativity. If we're positive and happy, we're contributing joy.

The universe wants us all to be happy and to enjoy ourselves. Not in a purely indulgent way, through smoking or drinking too much, but in a wholesome way, a good way. If we do that, we're making a really big contribution to life.

When we go into our heart, either in meditation or when we take a moment to connect to Source, we feel happier and more peaceful, and are making a contribution to others' happiness and peace. We're helping each other.

It's the same with beliefs about ageing. If we throw out negative beliefs and know that getting older is a positive process, we create almost unlimited years ahead for both ourselves and others. Know this and live as if it were true, because it *is* true.

People like Dr Hinohara, who had the secret of longevity, are showing us the way. And there are many ordinary people across the globe – just normal people, not doctors – who naturally know how to live for a very long time in good health and contentment. It's this knowing that is so important.

I talk about 'knowing' as opposed to 'believing' here, because they're different things. Belief is transient and fickle and changeable. For example, you might look back on beliefs you once held and think, *My goodness, I actually believed that!* It's okay to use belief at a certain stage – it's necessary as a sort of stepping stone – but, as I said earlier, a belief may or may not be the truth, and we should always be seeking the truth. The inspiring people who are living examples of vitality and longevity actually *know* how to live well. They're not in a belief system; they know, and that is the difference.

Take Antonio Todde, who in 2002, at the age of 112, held the record for the world's oldest man. A shepherd from Sardinia, he was in good health until he died just two weeks before his 113th birthday. When asked the secret of a long life, he said, 'Just love your brother and have a good glass of red wine every night.' When I heard this, I thought, *Wow*. I actually applauded when I saw that interview with him. To me, what he was saying was simply: 'Love everyone and enjoy yourself.' He probably didn't even realize at the time that he was saying such a wise, wonderful and deep-rooted thing. But did he believe he would grow infirm and enjoy life less as he got older? No.

Other supercentenarians give equally straightforward responses when asked how they've lived long and healthy lives. Richard Overton, 111, is currently not only America's oldest World War II veteran, but also the oldest man in the country. He's in good health and was still driving around his home city of Austin, Texas, at 110. (He had his licence renewed at 109, passing the eye test.) He smokes up to 12 cigars a day (he says he doesn't inhale), has a little whisky when he wants to and eats ice cream every night, because, he says, 'It makes me happy.'

Cigars, whisky and ice cream may not be the 'ideal' lifestyle choices for a supercentenarian, but there is a wholesomeness about enjoyment that seems to compensate for any negative effects.

Jamaican supercentenarian Violet Mosse Brown was officially recognized as the world's oldest person on 3 September 2017, when she was 117 years old. She died 12 days later. A former sugar plantation worker, she later became a business owner, growing and selling cane herself. She said that one reason for her longevity was her Christian faith. In her church, she had been the organist and director of the choir. Singing is the most beautiful thing. In a choir people are singing in harmony with each other, and this really enhances and enriches life.

Violet also said that her longevity was down to 'hard work'. Now, running a cane farm can't have been at all easy, and hard work in later life might sound like the last thing we want, especially when the media feeds us fantasies that the perfect retirement is taking a cruise and sipping a cocktail on a beach – in effect, doing nothing for the rest of our lives. But I know that's not the path to fulfilment. Whatever age we are, we need to be part of something meaningful – a community, a family, a profession – and to feel that we're making some contribution to the whole. We want to be looking to the future and have positive goals.

Teresa Hsu, a social worker and former nurse known as the 'Mother Teresa of Singapore', was still distributing food and money to the needy at 110 years old. She went on to live to 113. Born into a poor family in China, she recalled how her mother shared food with strangers – a mother and her children – who came to them and said they had not eaten for two days. Teresa founded two charities, Heart to Heart Services and the Home for the Aged Sick, in Singapore. She lived simply, had a vegetarian diet and an incredibly positive attitude to life.

She meditated, too. 'I spend a couple of hours every morning "clearing my brain" and focusing on the day ahead,' she said. 'I believe a healthy brain goes a long way towards living a long, quality life.'

When asked why she just didn't stay at home rather than go around supplying people with food, she replied that if she ate alone, she laughed alone, but if she shared food with 21 people, 21 people would laugh.

'You see,' she explained, 'my joy is multiplied 21 times.'

Good humour and laughter are such wonderful medicine. But what's also insightful here is that someone asked her, 'Why don't you just stay at home?' along with the unspoken, 'at your age…' That questioner was coming from the negative belief system about ageing that's so embedded in parts of our society. When we can change the collective consciousness around ageing, that question just won't be asked. It won't be part of our consciousness any more. Instead, people will be asking, 'Why are you staying at home? There's so much you can do!'

What They're Not Saying...

You may have noticed that in these accounts of healthy centenarians one thing is missing. That thing is money. Neither Shigeaki Hinohara, Antonio Todde, Violet Mosse Brown, Richard Overton nor Teresa Hsu mention money as the cause of their good health or contentment. Teresa Hsu lived very simply in a three-room apartment; she gave five apartments she inherited from her sister to house needy people. Richard Overton drove the same Ford truck for years because, he said, 'It runs just like I want it, so I just keep it.' We might imagine Dr Hinohara to have been comfortably off, with his medical and writing careers, but money was not his priority. 'The things that bring us deepest and lasting joy,' he said, 'are those that cannot be bought by money.'

In this sense, nothing is 'missing'. Whether they have money or not, these inspiring centenarians have love and purpose, and those are what counts.

While money is important for our basic security, it is not the answer. Money is just an energy; it's a resource rather than a goal.

Money was never a motivating force for Louise Hay, either. She founded the publishing company Hay House in 1984 with the goal of sharing her experience and wisdom through books. Money came with it, but it probably wouldn't have mattered to Louise if it hadn't. Her early work involved founding and running a weekly support group for people with AIDS and those affected by AIDS. The meetings began in January 1985 in her living room, with six people. These 'Hayrides', as they came to be known, were celebrations of the power of unconditional love, and the love grew until they had to move to an auditorium to accommodate the 200 people wanting to attend. The events were free of charge.

Louise inspired so many people to think positively; her landmark book, *You Can Heal Your Life*, has sold around 40 million copies. It links our thoughts and past experiences with physical ailments and helps us to create changes in our thinking that impact positively on our health.

Louise herself took up ballroom dancing in her mid-seventies. She'd wanted to dance for years, but had said, 'In the next lifetime, I'll be a dancer. It's too late to do it now.' But then she got a sign, literally – a dance studio with the notice: 'We teach you to dance one step at a time.' Encouraged, she thought: *I'm going to live quite a few more years – why am I waiting for the next lifetime?* She went on to dance every week.

She passed away recently, at the age of 90, having enjoyed many years of dancing and music. These things were her focus, rather than money.

I don't focus on money either. You might think, *That's all very well, Bill, with your salary,* but I've experienced ups and downs financially. I've had money and lost virtually everything, but recovered. So I know that while money can ease certain stresses in life, it is not a path to happiness. Anyone who has been through very difficult times knows this. They know that when they have lost someone close to them and are grieving, money is no comfort. When we lost Edwina, our lovely home didn't change how we were feeling, and why would it? Money cannot and should not insulate us from feeling what needs to be felt.

Money, as they say, can't buy you happiness, and it can't guarantee a long, healthy life either. That comes from having a positive, loving attitude and purpose, and knowing that you can live for a long time. I know that there are those with serious money problems which need to be resolved. But if you are living within your income, whatever that is, then you are well off.

My work gives me that vital sense of involvement and purpose. While I don't in any way compare the work I do to that of Dr Hinohara, Violet Mosse Brown, Richard Overton or Teresa Hsu, I know that belonging to the *Coronation Street* family contributes to my wellbeing. It's a challenge – learning lines can be tough – but playing scenes with others can be pure harmony. My work overall always feels worthwhile, because it gives me both personal goals and a collective purpose.

Coronation Street was conceived as social drama portraying the lives of ordinary people. It's never waved a flag, telling people what they should or shouldn't do, but many of its storylines have reached out to people in need of support, and I'm proud to have been a part of that. Over the years we've had some fantastic storylines that have helped raise awareness of important social issues, too, and, I hope, changed people's perceptions.

When Ken had his stroke earlier this year, we hoped the story would raise awareness of stroke, for example, and, as I said earlier, we worked hard to make sure we got the portrayal accurate. We've also had Steve McDonald (Simon Gregson) offering a moving insight into depression and anxiety. The producers worked closely with the mental health charity MIND for those episodes. Then we had Izzy Armstrong (Cherylee Houston) trying to get cannabis for pain relief to highlight the struggles of people with long-term conditions who want to use cannabis without fear of prosecution. There was also the relationship between two much-loved characters, Roy and Hayley Cropper, when Julie Hesmondhalgh played the world's first transsexual character in a serialized drama.

We do things as truthfully as possible, and I like the fact that we have that responsibility. Whether I've been in any of those scenes or not doesn't matter – what's important is that I'm part of the cast and the *Coronation Street* family.

Attitude to Diet

I know my reasonably balanced diet will probably help me live longer than I otherwise would, but there's no magic chemical formula that makes the body keep on going. It's all about having a positive attitude, having purpose and staying connected. There are, of course, basic principles, as I explained in the last chapter, but you could tie yourself in knots if you followed everything that's out there that's supposed to extend your lifespan. Of the centenarians and supercentenarians I know of, none seems to have a complicated dietary regime. Some enjoy alcohol, some don't. You can have a glass of wine a day, as Antonio Todde says, if you choose to do so. It's all about moderation and, importantly, enjoyment. These people do seem to follow what's right for them, though, and if they like doing something, they keep doing it.

While many researchers continue to investigate the diet of healthy older people, there's no agreed 'longevity diet' at all. It seems to me that the people living in areas renowned for longevity are just keeping it simple and eating what's fresh and available. On the Okinawa Islands in Japan, which the Chinese refer to as the 'Land of the Immortals', the diet consists of wholegrains, indigenous vegetables, seafood, including seaweed, and soya. In Loma Linda in California, the relatively long and healthy lives of residents are attributed to a mainly vegetarian diet. In Sardinia, land of my happiness hero Antonio Todde, they eat a Mediterranean diet, including local cheeses that promote good gut bacteria.

What I can say for sure is that while the diets of these healthy older people are nutritious, there's something else in play, too: what strikes me is that in their societies, very senior citizens are considered worth talking to. They're included and consulted, and have a real place in the family and wider community. They're not seen as oddities because they've lived a long time; reaching 100 years is normal in these towns and villages. And there's no point at which older people there somehow become invisible or useless. On the contrary, they are respected for their wisdom.

This is so important, because, as I've said, our collective and cultural beliefs about ageing determine whether or not we have a long and healthy life. When we believe and accept that living to 100 and beyond is normal, it becomes normal. And when older people stay part of the community, with a role and a purpose, it helps everyone.

I was struck by the truth of this recently while watching a Channel 4 documentary, *Old People's Home for 4 Year Olds*, in which 10 residents in a care home near Bristol in the west of England were put together with 10 pre-school children to assess how interacting with them might benefit their health and happiness.

At the beginning of the experiment, many of the residents said they felt they had little to look forward to, and all felt physically vulnerable, concerned about falling. During the six weeks of the experiment, the adults and children had lots of fun – everything from blowing up balloons and seeing chicks hatch to joining in a sports day. The children didn't judge the older people negatively. They wanted them to join in with all their games and saw them as equals, as people who could talk to them and learn with them. Over time, the children and the residents began teaching each other, and the residents began to remember who they were – their true selves, before limited mobility or negativity or bereavement became a big part of their consciousness.

The residents were tested for depression, grip strength, activity levels and how long it took them to get up from a chair, walk three metres and go back to the chair (the 'get up and go' test used to assess mobility). And as they made a connection with the children, their wellbeing improved. Seventy per cent of the group had improved scores for mood and depression by the end of the experiment, and 80 per cent had improved grip strength and mobility.

Without this kind of stimulation, people stagnate. I saw this with my mother. At 95, she was living on her own. When she fell and broke her hip, she wasn't really able to look after herself, so she went into a residential home. The first week I went there, she was walking around, organizing things. Two weeks later, she was still fairly active, but not doing as much. A couple of weeks after that, she was sitting there with the other residents, and she fell into that pattern very quickly because she had no purpose. In her mind, and in everybody else's mind, she had gone there to die. And the place had that feel about it. It was all about the collective thinking.

Bringing children into a care home is like shining a golden beam onto that collective thinking to dissolve it. It changes everything. It's a brilliant idea, and already established in America. In Seattle, for example, the Intergenerational Learning Center is a nursing home that shares its space with over 100 young children five days a week.

In the care home in Bristol, I could really see how the children's energy, radiance, enthusiasm and positivity affected everybody. It was better than any vitamin pills or anything else you could prescribe. One gentleman with mobility problems – he'd lost a leg early on in life – had been sceptical about the experiment at first, but the children soon got him out of his chair on the floor playing sleeping lions. He was roaring at them and they were shrieking with laughter. It was a great example of how someone can quickly open up, be in harmony with others and be in touch with positive and enthusiastic energy.

Another US study into wellbeing in a care home showed the benefits of small, purposeful acts in a very simple way. As part of her research into mindfulness and ageing, Harvard psychology professor Ellen Langer encouraged one group of residents at a nursing home in Connecticut to do a few tasks every day, such as making a cup of tea and tending a houseplant. Eighteen months later, they were more positive in their outlook and more alert and active than the residents who hadn't taken part in the trial. They lived longer, too.

It's all about having some purpose! It doesn't matter if it's making a cup of tea or watering a plant, having something positive to do has very positive results.

Langer also conducted a 'counterclockwise' study, in which she took a group of men in their late seventies and early eighties to a retreat and 'retro-fitted' it as if it were 20 years in the past. The men had to live and speak as if they were in that time. After one week they looked younger, and their hearing, sight, memory and physical strength had all improved. Again, it ultimately goes back to what you believe. Age is a state of mind.

Of course you might say, 'That's all very well, but what about genes?' Neuropsychologist Dr Mario Martinez, a researcher into the impact of cultural beliefs and the connection between mind and body on health and ageing, suggests that genes may account for only 20 per cent of our health and longevity. Dr Bruce Lipton, stem cell biologist and author of *The Biology of Belief*, says only 1 per cent of genes actually account for inherited disease. Just 1 per cent!

Centenarian Consciousness

Martinez believes you can change your beliefs and learn to live longer at any age. He calls this 'centenarian consciousness'. This belief is seen in the common expression from Sardinia, a country renowned for longevity, '*A kent'annos*', which means, 'May you live 100 years.'

Just think how we could change negative beliefs about ageing by saying this. Repeating this greeting day after day could help change our collective consciousness.

Martinez noticed the following traits in the hundreds of healthy centenarians he studied on his travels across the globe:

Healthy centenarians are assertive

'They know how to set limits, which is good for the immune system,' he says. They also have 'righteous anger, which is getting angry about appropriate things', and this is also good for the immune system. (Being angry all the time is bad for the immune system.)

This accords with my views, too. It's important to put yourself first, to value your time, whether you're working or not, whether you're busy or not, and say 'no' when you need to. With anger, it's okay to be angry if, say, the government or society is harming someone and no one's doing anything about it. Yes, be angry, then use the anger to do something positive about it!

Healthy centenarians have 'healthy narcissism'

This is narcissism that is inclusive. For example, one of the centenarians Martinez observed exclaimed, 'Did you notice how the women were looking at me? They love me. I'm so damned good-looking. But you notice how beautiful they are? They can see I'm beautiful because they're beautiful.'

I loved this man's attitude. He complimented himself and included the women around him at the same time. We're all beautiful. Every human being is beautiful, and the human body is a wonderful instrument. We need to appreciate ourselves and enjoy our beauty, saying, 'Yes I am beautiful, I am marvellous.' Each one of us is a living miracle.

Healthy centenarians don't want to talk about being ill

This is so important. Unfortunately, many older people can get drawn into never-ending conversations about their health and that of their peers. Little moans and complaints can dominate entire conversations.

Of course we have to talk about how we are from time to time, but don't let this become the focal point of a conversation. Instead of talking about ill-health and bad weather (the two seem to somehow go together), talk about the future and things that you enjoy. Focus on the good things in life. This is a habit you can develop quite quickly, and it does get results. You feel more positive and optimistic, and begin to look at what's right with the world rather than what's wrong.

Healthy centenarians do have much to teach us and, as Martinez says, we can learn a lot from them.

Looking Closer to Home

I've included some wonderful people in this chapter who've done great things, but there are inspirational people on our doorstep as well – well, maybe not literally, but pretty close to where we live. We might see them at the supermarket, or on the street, or they may be part of an existing circle of friends or acquaintances. They could be the woman we see cycling every day or the man walking his dogs at a brisk pace – in fact, we might not consider them role models for ageing at first, because they don't seem old or infirm at all.

Noticing Positive Ageing

Look around and you'll see someone who is bright-eyed and pretty well ready to laugh most of the time; they're really healthy, and enjoying themselves, too. They're an inspiration to you, whatever age you are!

If you go up and talk to them, you'll find they have more positive things to say than negative. They may not be on a diet or doing strict gym workouts, but they will get a reasonable amount of exercise and fresh air. They'll know what good food is and they will enjoy it, and they'll indulge themselves with a few treats now and again, but they'll have life in balance. They'll have a feeling of being connected, of caring for other people, for animals, for the Earth and, above all, for themselves.

These people just stand out; it's in the eyes. Notice them and consider them your inspiration, your mentors.

You'll also see people who aren't like this. If you speak to them, they may focus on ailments and hospital appointments. But negative talk, as I've said, builds up a negative belief system and sends energy levels plummeting. So, when our cells renew themselves, they renew themselves with this lower energy, and so the ageing process goes on.

To inspire you now, here are just a few examples of yet more ordinary people who have achieved extraordinary goals. In time, as our collective beliefs about ageing become more positive, these achievements won't seem so extraordinary. We'll come to applaud and accept them the same way we do the achievements of people of any age; the fact that they are in later life won't be as significant. But in the here and now, these inspirational people share a very positive knowing: they know that getting older doesn't mean frailty or illness. In fact, some of them have become fitter and healthier as the years have passed.

Ernestine Shepherd, 81, is an American bodybuilder and personal trainer from Baltimore. At 56, she and her sister, Velvet, took up aerobics, then began bodybuilding and entering competitions. In 2010, Ernestine was named the world's oldest competitive bodybuilder. She also took up running, has run nine marathons and currently runs 80 or so miles each week. She is inspired by a quote from American self-help author Og Mandino, which came to her via her sister: 'Welcome every morning with a smile. Look on the new day as another special gift from your Creator, another golden opportunity to complete what you were unable to finish yesterday.'

Charles Eugster, a British dentist, began bodybuilding at 87 because he believed it was possible to get a 'beach body' in older age – and he achieved it. He had been an athlete when he was younger, but his sporting activities had slowed down when he got married and had children. His secrets to a long and healthy life included working, good nutrition and, of course, exercise. He lived in Switzerland and had a multitude of sporting trophies, including awards for rowing and bodybuilding. Before he died, aged 97, he said, 'People can start a new life, a new job, rebuild their bodies, whatever their age.' If you check out Charles' TEDx talk, recorded in Zurich in 2012 when he was 93, you'll see that he was sharp, funny and inspiring. His presentation is a real battle cry for older people, and a reminder to us all, whatever age we may be, of what we can achieve with positive thinking and a sense of purpose.

Johanna Quaas, a 92-year-old German gymnast and coach, has been training since she was 10 years old. In 2012, when she was 86, she became the oldest gymnast in the world, certified by Guinness World Records after performing a routine in Rome, Italy. She trains for one hour a day, usually swimming or walking, and practises gymnastics twice a week. She doesn't take pills, has a healthy diet with lots of fruit and vegetables, and is in good health. She says, 'My face is old, but my heart is young.'

Our body is a wonderful vehicle. Science can't make a robot anything like a human being. We have everything we need within us to cure disease: we're imaginative, we're creative, we can run, talk, cook, build, read, interact and play sport. Our body facilitates the enjoyment that is our life.

With its ever-renewing cells, the body was originally designed to last as long we wanted it to. When the soul decided it wanted to go home, it went. The body didn't deteriorate through age; this came about through our free will, as a result of which we have behaved in an unloving way, eaten the wrong sorts of food and not been connected to the wonderful harmony of the universe. Over time, this has begun to close us down and placed limitations on how long we will live. This closing down, or disconnection from Source, has also brought disease, which is, as we know, 'dis-ease', or stress. I know this is what has curtailed our years on the planet.

Science, however, takes a different view. Through genetic engineering, scientists are seeking to reduce or eradicate certain diseases and conditions associated with ageing, thereby increasing our 'health span' – the number of years we're healthy – as well as extending our lifespan.

Scientists at the Mayo Clinic in Minnesota, USA, for example, have been able to extend the lifespan of middle-aged mice. They tweaked part of the mice's genetic code, then injected them with a specific drug so that their senescent cells were destroyed. Without these cells, the mice lived up to 25 per cent longer than normal, and they stayed healthier. Senescent cells exist in people, too – they are living cells, but they no longer reproduce, and we get more of them as we age. They act upon the body in a variety of ways – while they can help suppress tumours, they may also contribute to age-related conditions such as chronic inflammation, Type 2 diabetes and kidney failure.

Further research into removing senescent cells in mice at Erasmus University Medical Centre in the Netherlands showed that this gene tweak could potentially reverse ageing – mice that were treated regrew their hair, became more energetic and lived up to 20 per cent longer on average.

Then there are the researchers at Albert Einstein College of Medicine in New York who are looking to implant stem cells into the human brain. Stem cells, found in the brain's hypothalamus, die off as we age (by the time we reach middle age, there are barely any left), so implanting fresh ones could slow down the ageing process.

Molecular biologist Cynthia Kenyon at the University of California, San Francisco, discovered that partially disabling a single gene, 'daf-2', in roundworms doubled their normal lifespan and they stayed healthy until they died. When she gave the worms a bit of sugar, it shortened their lifespan. What makes this relevant to humans is that we have two genes that are like daf-2, and by manipulating these, scientists could potentially program us to have longer, healthier lives.

Yet even if scientists learn how to manufacture new genes, they may be influencing only 20 per cent of our ability to stay healthy for longer, as Dr Martinez suggests, or less, as Bruce Lipton says. I know that the remaining 80 per cent (at least) comes from connecting with Source and understanding what and who we are. As we begin to live in harmony with this knowing, to eat well and care for ourselves naturally, our genes will change. We will embody our thinking and live longer, healthier lives as a result.

Of course, while scientists of course do very valuable work, they are not the inspirational people who will lead us back to the long and healthy life that was our original inheritance. The current research is an expression of our Western scientific approach: we are investing millions of dollars into finding the elixir of life, regardless of the fact that there are people living very long lives without ground-breaking longevity drugs or gene manipulation. Scientists are playing catch-up with nature and creation. They show glimpses of how it can be, and help us to remember and understand how we should live, so they do make a great contribution, but the real answers lie within us.

These great truths are already understood by all of us. Deep within, we all have the heartfelt knowing that we are all love, and we can live long lives in good health and be happy and at peace, in harmony with ourselves and with nature. We don't need a PhD to recognize this. In fact, great intelligence can actually make life very difficult, because then we believe that the intellect is the seat of power and where the answers are. So, yes, scientists do great work, but they are only finding out little bits of truth, and they don't know everything. As I said, they're playing catch-up. Like all of us, they have forgotten who they are.

If we seek the truth, we can remember who we are: the energy of love. As I said earlier, everything is made from love. There is nothing in existence that is not love.

This may be very hard to accept, but it is true. Even what we call 'bad' and 'evil' is still the energy of love, it's just that it has become distorted and disconnected from Source. It has not only forgotten where it has come from, but it has also forgotten that it has forgotten. So there is little attempt to regain the truth, and this is the cause of humanity's dangerous predicament.

But if we can remember that we are love, we can start to express ourselves as loving beings – loving each other, loving the Earth, loving the Source of our life and, importantly, loving ourselves. And as we do this, we will release the negative beliefs that ageing means frailty and ill-health. We will come to know that we can live to any age we choose and enjoy a life that is rich, rewarding, healthy and happy.

As more and more people make this positive leap in consciousness, our genes will change accordingly and generations to come will inherit this knowing. We will live not just to 100 years, but to 200 and more, healthy, happy and in harmony with everything around us.

Chapter 7

LIVING IN
THE PRESENT

One of reasons I'm generally relaxed and content is probably how I see time. To me, it is purely a measuring system. In itself it doesn't do anything; it is neither good nor bad, it just is. The sun comes up, the sun goes down, and we gauge our lives by it. Time helps us to create order and helps to avoid chaos. But that's all it is – a way of measuring. It's up to us whether we get pressurized about it or load it with too much importance.

In the other realms, time doesn't exist, but they do have sequence and process. So that's where I put my focus in this realm – on what I'm doing and how to do it. When I was working on this book, all I thought was, *We've got this book to do, there's a timeframe, and that will help us organize the process*. I didn't allow pressure in.

If I think there isn't enough time to do something, I talk about it. I deal with it. Otherwise, I'm facing it on my own, in my head, and negative thoughts can take root: *What if I can't do it? What if time runs out?* In that respect, time is a bit like electricity. We need it to help things run, but too much leads to an overload of current, stress on the system, and shock or panic. In these situations I find it's always helpful to remember what time truly is – just a measuring instrument that helps us to organize our lives effectively. And we can be grateful for it rather than fear it.

The Sacred Present

The perceived pressure of time can affect us at all ages, but some people feel the passing of time more keenly as they age and feel fearful about the future. As I said earlier, there is a collective belief that ageing is synonymous with frailty, illness and death within a certain parameter of years. But that is all it is: a belief. And because it's a belief it can be challenged, and our physical lifetime extended.

So, rather than think, *I don't know how much time I've got/ There's no point starting that novel/moving house/learning to fly/I'll never manage this project because I won't have the time or energy*, we can say to ourselves, *I'm going to live long enough and have enough energy to do whatever I choose.* When we think like this, we're not only creating change in our own life, but challenging a collective belief about ageing, health and time. We're pushing parameters and helping to create a more positive reality for others.

Of course we all have to die sometime, but we go when we're ready. Our soul knows when that is, and that's when we go. And when we do pass on, we go to a far better place than here: we go home. It's like being taken home from school.

If I do have the occasional stray thought about ageing that's negative, I just go into my heart and feel the oneness of our eternal nature. I feel relaxed, at ease and calm in myself – and not distracted by external pressures or demands. The fear of not having enough time to do what we need to do creates stress and pressure, and this perception comes from the mind, not from the heart. Think, *Oh, I haven't got time*, and you immediately restrict time. Like attracts like. Negative thinking creates negative outcomes.

When you quietly go into your heart, there is no fear, no worry that time is running out. You feel completely in the present moment and aren't worrying about the future or thinking about the past.

And that's pretty much how I am on a day-to-day basis. I live in the present as much as I can. As I've mentioned, that's not because I fear the future at all, because I fear dying – far from it. It's because the here and now is the only time we can do anything. I call this 'the sacred present'.

It's sacred because in the present moment, we are our true selves. And that's the only time we *can* be our true selves.

Being our true selves means experiencing oneness with the All That Is – oneness with everything and everyone – and that can only happen when we're living in, and responding to, the present moment; when we are present to who we truly are.

At that moment, we don't feel stressed or agitated or under pressure. Depending on what we're doing, we may have no sense of time passing, either. When we're doing something we really enjoy, such as a creative hobby or sport, we're not thinking about the past or the future. We could probably spend all day doing it and not realize that time has flown by. On the other hand, when we're not enjoying something, time drags. When we're resisting where we are and what we're doing, every moment can feel like an hour. But when we accept whatever the present moment brings and are open to what might happen, amazing things can occur. And being in the here and now really supports our wellbeing; there's no resistance, no stress. We're able to make good decisions, looking at what's important right now, from a calm centre.

It's actually pretty easy to get in the present. It's just a matter of paying attention to exactly what we're doing when we're doing it rather than letting our mind skip ahead.

Now I know what I'm going to say may sound like a contradiction, but here it is: when we're focusing on one thing, other thoughts are able to come in – creative, expansive thoughts. By getting singular in our thinking – say by just concentrating on filling the kettle or putting on our shoes – we somehow free up our mind, and our awareness becomes more expansive. We become more creative, more imaginative, more relaxed. It's a great technique to call upon whenever we feel anxious or stressed, because we can suddenly go into that liberating, creative space. It's like flicking a switch.

If we're faced with a pile of work or a problem that seems overwhelming and think, *I can't get into this, I can't understand it*, we've gone into a totally negative thought that's not helping us. But if we focus on one little bit of that work or one part of that problem, we release ourselves from the negative thinking. 'A journey of 1,000 miles starts with a single step' is an old adage, but it works. It's just about getting present to what we're doing and doing it. Then we tackle the next bit, and the next, and we're off. It gets easier, and we begin to see our way through it – and may even get a flash of insight along the way.

I use this technique for work, say if I've got a big scene coming up and lots of lines to learn. I learned this in my early acting days. Instead of looking at pages and pages of script and thinking, *I'll never learn all this*, I'd just take the first page and learn the first words. That's all it would take to get going, and I learned to use this approach for any situation.

When we're anxious or under pressure, doing is far more important than thinking. People don't realize how harmful negative thinking is. If we start thinking negatively about anything, we're weakening ourselves and distracting ourselves and thinking ourselves down.

So, when you're getting all anxious and you're trying to do all sorts of things at once, just say, 'No, I'll focus just on what I'm doing.' And you'll find tremendous relief and a tremendous release of energy in doing that.

Of course, we all get caught up in worrying about the future sometimes, anticipating what it is to come in a negative way. But when we arrive at the situation we've been worrying about, we almost invariably think, *Hang on – this isn't as bad as I thought it was going to be.* It's worth remembering that.

So, try not to feel stressed about future outcomes and instead just focus on what you're doing now. This doesn't mean you can't think about the future and the past – it's natural to do this. But what's exciting is that you can be in the here and now, feeling really present, and then look at the past and future in a creative, inspirational way, rather than a negative, worrying way. And this will be easy, because when you're in the present moment and are your sacred true self, your divine self, you naturally look at things in a more positive way, a more creative way, a more beautiful way and a more loving way. So getting into the moment is a wonderful way to step into your own divinity.

STEPPING INTO YOUR TRUE SELF

In this exercise, you step into your truth by stepping outside yourself and observing what's going on. You see the bigger picture and have a better understanding of what's going on in your life right now, and you can observe your past and your future without regret or fear.

- *Take a deep breath and go into your heart (see page 26). Feel that sense of expansion and peace as it comes in, little by little.*

- *When you are ready, allow yourself to move towards the future. Imagine that you are watching yourself from a distance and seeing yourself doing this. What do you feel? If you feel anxious, it's your mind getting in the way, so take a breath, go back into your heart and then step back into the observer position. As the observer, you are your true loving self, and in the future, your true self knows no fear or negativity. It's always peaceful and it's always positive.*

- *If you choose, you can now look back into your past. What is there for you? If you feel any remorse or guilt, let it go. You did what you did; you can understand and maybe learn from some mistakes that you made and then go forwards. There is no guilt in the past, only experience. The you that is the observer knows this. The observer is the true you and the real you.*

When we are in touch with our eternal selves, we feel our soul's guidance. And that guidance leads us not only to new opportunities, but to understanding when it's right to stay in existing situations, too. I talk a lot about being in our true self, but actually this is the same as our intuition or conscience. We should learn to trust our intuition much more.

Whatever I've done in life, I've always stayed on a bit longer than other people. That seems to be part of the pattern of my life. It's not been down to circumstances, but who I am. If I'm challenged and I'm happy, I don't see any reason to change the status quo. I stayed on at school for an additional year to get the qualifications I needed for medical school. When I was in the army, I extended my national service by taking a short service commission, and reached the rank of Captain. Later, I volunteered for the Trucial Oman Scouts in the Persian Gulf; that lasted another two years. When I considered acting, I thought about drama school and knew that at 25, I'd probably left it too late. But I persevered, because something was driving me onwards. I now know that this was my soul wisdom, my higher self or intuition, telling me it wasn't too late and to never give up. I had a calling, and I didn't think about failure, or what the future might hold, I just got on with what I had to do. I'd go to the cinema in London, near my bedsit in Earl's Court, and then write to the director of the film I'd seen, asking for work. This continued for months and I wrote hundreds of letters.

I finally landed a role with the famous Irish director Brian Desmond Hurst. The film was *Behind the Mask*, and I played an anaesthetist – the drama was about surgeons. Given that my first calling was to follow my father into medicine, this was a nice synchronicity.

That role, along with further small film parts, led on to weekly repertory theatre, or rep. I joined Oldham Rep. and had to learn and perform a play a week – anything from Shakespeare to pantomime. It was wonderful experience, playing so many different characters in front of a live audience. I barely took any time off at all, and by the end of it my brain was numb from the speed of turnaround and tackling a new script every week. I never thought about leaving, though, until my wife at the time, Anna, said, 'Bill, don't do too much of this, it's bad for you.' This made me move. Otherwise I know I would have carried on.

Of course there can be a downside to staying put, but there will always be a positive and a negative aspect to any situation. Whatever I've done in my career, I've stayed because it felt right and because I was enjoying it. And what a surprise – I stayed in *Coronation Street*, too! I'm actually in the *Guinness World Records* as the longest-serving actor in an ongoing drama, having been in the Street for more than 58 years. We didn't call it soap originally, of course; it was cutting-edge drama, then part of the new realism sweeping through the acting profession. We were the first kitchen sink drama.

The other aspect of staying on in situations and roles is that I always want to do things to the best of my ability, and it takes time to learn something and do it well. And because I'm present to what I'm doing, thinking just about what I'm doing when I'm doing it, I see the positives all the time. I'm not thinking about what else is around the corner, I'm just enjoying what I have to do. This is part of who I am, my essence and my soul, which is lovely, because what it probably means is that I'll live a long time. Maybe I could live to be 100 or 120 and still be in good health. I'm certainly open to that!

Endurance is important to me in other ways, too. When I bought a Rolls-Royce, it wasn't for effect – 'Oh, he's got a

Rolls-Royce!' – it was because the Rolls lasts longer than any other car, and mine wasn't even a new one! I like old buildings, too, because they are stone-built and solid; I've always loved things that are built to last.

My home has always been a great anchor for me; I've been here more than 35 years now. It's not a mansion – it has five bedrooms plus the conservatory, where I enjoy my quiet time each day. The house and garden are easy to manage, and there's space for the family to come up and stay. It's where Verity and Will were brought up, and of course where Sara and I were together all those years. But I'm happy here on my own. I like it, it's comfortable and I'm happy to stay where I am!

Valuing Your Time

I know my time is important to me, and I value it. I may be pictured at social events – award ceremonies, things like that – but the truth is I'm pretty much a private person and I like time on my own.

I am also careful about how I spend my time. Maybe that's because I am naturally reserved – hard to believe of an actor, but it's true. While I do like people, basically I'm not very sociable. There, I've said it. I don't really enjoy glamorous parties with lots of people I don't know, and I don't spend my evenings round the dinner table with other well-known people, even though I do seem to attract dinner-party invitations. If I accept on just one occasion, though, I have to watch out in case some kind of expectation develops, because I don't want to hurt people's feelings. One really nice friend and her husband kept asking me to dinner because she thought they were doing me a favour. I had to tell her straight, in the end, that I just don't like dinner parties and big social occasions. Once I confessed, she was absolutely fine about it. We're still friends, and now she understands me better, too.

This doesn't mean I'm a hermit. I go to charity events organized by John Hayes and his company, Champions, because I support and admire the work that John and those charities do, and I enjoy every event. I play golf, and that's fun and great exercise. I travel, occasionally, and meet regularly with a group that I'm part of, and we have great camaraderie. We don't make too much small talk, but we do have great conversations about making the world a better place. And I do like a great many people. I like the whole cast of *Coronation Street*, but we don't meet up socially.

Whenever I do choose to go out, I'm present when I'm there, and that's what matters to me. I'm sure you'll recall meeting people who just seem to be somewhere else – they're looking over your shoulder, they're constantly on their iPhone or whatever, and they don't make much eye contact. You see them in restaurants, too – on the phone during a meal rather than talking to the person they're with. Maybe they don't want to be there. Maybe they're feeling pressured by work, or other commitments, or whatever. But they're not present in the room, and you can't help but wonder why they turned up in the first place.

Saying 'no' to things we don't want to do or don't have time for isn't being selfish, it's being self-aware. By saying 'no' when we need to, we're saving our energy and looking after ourselves properly. Of course, this isn't always easy, because we don't want to upset people, but it's important to be true to ourselves. We don't need to let other people and their arrangements sap our life away. Our time is precious. I know, at least for me, that it's vital to spend my time how I choose.

True friends always understand this. They're not demanding, and they're there for us whether we're with them often or rarely. I have several great friends I've known for years. They make no demands, I see them now and again, and I know if I didn't see them for 12 months, that would be perfectly okay. We've never been in each other's pockets, and we don't have to be, because we fundamentally understand one another.

I don't seek a great many close friends, but I really value those I do have. I count my manager as both family and friend – we're in touch lots, and he is a regular part of my life, a constant. That has been really important to me. When Sara died, he stepped in straight away and managed things that she had previously taken care of, and during the court case, as you know, he was amazing.

Some people profess to care about us, but we know that they really do when they're willing to sacrifice their time and energy to help us. Words are easy, whereas actions are a manifestation of our friendship and our love.

That's something that's worth considering if you're ever thinking about the friends you have around you. Invest your time with people who do what they say they'll do and with whom you can be yourself. With those people, there's no 'deal' or contract – 'You do this and I'll do that in return' – you just tell each other the truth, and you follow it through. True friendship is undemanding, and it's a beautiful feeling of absolute freedom. You don't need to analyze it. It comes from the heart.

It's simple, really – there are people we have an affinity with and those we don't. And it's very natural and sensible to associate with the people who make us feel relaxed and happy.

First and foremost, though, the most important relationship we all have is with ourselves. We have to look after ourselves and not do things that are alien to our personality. Everything we do should be uplifting, joyful and full of life and have a good energy about it.

Here's a test question: if you could magically remove yourself from a situation or person without any upset to anybody, what or who would it be? If you include family and relationships, that's a dangerous party game to play…! But seriously, I'd say a lot of people in unhappy romantic relationships might choose to magically disappear!

I do think that a lot of us, if we were honest, would remove ourselves instantly from certain situations. But I'm smiling to myself as I write this, because I know how much easier it can be to say 'yes' to something rather than risk hurting someone's feelings. It requires great strength of character to say 'no', and most of us are just too nice. We sense that certain people or situations will drain us, but we go along with them anyway – and sure enough, our energy is depleted.

I love everybody, I genuinely do, in the sense that I really care about everybody, but I don't choose to spend time with everyone. I don't want this to sound as though I advocate hurting people who reach out to me, but whom we choose to be with and what we choose to do in life will either give us energy and joy or it will sap our vitality. So we need to put ourselves first in a positive way, and know when to step away and say 'no' in order to keep ourselves as vigorous and energetic as we want to be.

PUTTING YOURSELF FIRST

Imagine that you've just taken over a new business. That new business needs to flow, so you've got to remove what isn't helpful. It's the same with your life!

Make some notes:

- *What is enhancing your life? Think about regular social commitments, individuals or groups you spend time with.*

- *What's become a habit? How do you feel afterwards – relaxed or drained?*

- *What or whom is dragging you down?*

Be really, really truthful with yourself when you're doing this exercise – no one is going to see what you write.

When you're more aware of what supports you and what drains you, you can look at reducing the time you spend in draining situations. Being constantly drained can make you ill eventually. Choose what invigorates and supports you and don't feel bad about it. I call this being 'positively and lovingly selfish'! But it's not selfish really – when you love yourself, you're also in a better position to love others.

SUMMARY: LIVING IN THE PRESENT

- If you don't have enough time to do something, talk about it rather than worry alone.

- Rather than feel fearful about the future, think positively and tell yourself you will have the time and energy to do what you want. Know that you will only go to your eternal home when your soul knows you're ready.

- Live in the present moment as much as you can. That's where you are your true self.

- When faced with a lot to do, focus on the first bit and begin. Then keep going.

- Allow your intuition to guide you when to take up new opportunities and when to stay where you are.

- Value your time and be careful how you spend it. Love yourself and enjoy yourself, and then you can benefit others, too.

CONCLUSION

We are all beings of love. We're here to learn and to express ourselves, and we can be in charge of how we live our lives. The best way is to live according to our true nature.

We open up to that true nature by thinking from our heart. When we go into our heart, we connect with the one energy of which we're all made, the pure love of Source. We can bring that love out into our daily life in small ways that can make a big difference.

The Daily Plan

- Meditate for five minutes, twice a day. Go into your heart and connect with Source and your true self.

- Try to take in as much positive information as you can.

Watch TV programmes that are uplifting and make you laugh. Don't engage in negative conversations or adopt negative belief systems. Keep your outlook positive every day.

- Accept compliments with grace, rather than denying them with 'What? No!' or 'Really?' Instead, just say 'Thank you.'

- Be grateful for all the great things you have and enjoy. The important things are often the little ones. Don't take them for granted. Appreciate the small stuff and you open yourself up to greater things later on.

- Be in tune with yourself by being in your heart. This keeps stress at bay and helps you to make good decisions about everything, including eating nourishing food and taking the right exercise.

- If fear and anxiety come in, just stop. Take a breath and go into your heart, into peace and love. Think of somewhere that makes you feel relaxed and peaceful.

- Tackle boring jobs quickly rather than letting them build up, as they just block the flow of life.

- Make time for yourself and put yourself first. This is really important. You need space to be in tune with yourself. And by keeping yourself relaxed and happy, you will be better company when with other people.

- Look for agreement, not conflict. What connects you? There's always a connection to build on. Looking for differences just creates conflict. Learn to discuss rather than argue, and be a good listener.

- Laugh as much as you can. Laughter is a great healer.

- Keep life simple. If things feel complicated, you're probably in your head, not your heart.

- Be present. This moment, now, is the point at which you are empowered. Look after the present and the future will take care of itself.

Above all, love everyone and enjoy yourself.

POSTSCRIPT

This book was finished and about to go to print when my eldest daughter, Vanya, died on 2 March 2018. She was only 50 years old. The shock and grief is immeasurable.

We only had just over two weeks in which to arrange her funeral, and we decided to hold the service ourselves at the crematorium. This kept us occupied. It is good to grieve for a while because you miss your loved one, but also good, as soon as you can, to get to the stage where you think about the happy times. Because we were holding the service ourselves, we decided that it should be a celebration of Vanya's life and an expression of our love for her, and we quickly became able to think about the happy times. And I know that she is now dancing in a wonderful place.

ABOUT THE AUTHOR

William Roache MBE is one of Britain's most beloved actors, best known for his long-running portrayal of Ken Barlow in the popular British TV serial *Coronation Street*.

With more than 58 years as a TV star under his belt, Bill didn't always want to be an actor. He intended to follow in his father's footsteps and become a doctor, but was called up for national service and only turned to acting upon leaving the army. Bill learned the craft of acting during two years in repertory theatre, performing to live audiences. Film and TV roles followed, and he joined the cast of *Coronation Street* in 1960. Bill appeared in the very first episode of the show and has now appeared consistently for more than 58 years.

In 2000 he was given a Lifetime Achievement Award at the British Television Soap Awards, and he holds a Guinness World Record as the longest-serving actor in an ongoing drama. Bill gained the highest honour in 2001 when, as part of the Queen's New Year's Honours, he was awarded an MBE for his services to television drama and work as an actor. He also holds an Honorary Doctor of Letters degree from the University of Chester, and an Honorary MA from the University of Derby.

Outside of his work as a professional actor, Bill is known for his interest in the meaning of life and seeking the great truths that never change. Family is of the highest importance to him, and he is the proud father of five children. Two of his sons have also gone on to become actors in their own right.

Bill lives in Wilmslow, Cheshire. This is his third book.

Hay House Podcasts
Bring Fresh, Free Inspiration Each Week!

Hay House proudly offers a selection of life-changing audio content via our most popular podcasts!

Hay House Meditations Podcast

Features your favorite Hay House authors guiding you through meditations designed to help you relax and rejuvenate. Take their words into your soul and cruise through the week!

Dr. Wayne W. Dyer Podcast

Discover the timeless wisdom of Dr. Wayne W. Dyer, world-renowned spiritual teacher and affectionately known as "the father of motivation." Each week brings some of the best selections from the 10-year span of Dr. Dyer's talk show on HayHouseRadio.com.

Hay House World Summit Podcast

Over 1 million people from 217 countries and territories participate in the massive online event known as the Hay House World Summit. This podcast offers weekly mini-lessons from World Summits past as a taste of what you can hear during the annual event, which occurs each May.

Hay House Radio Podcast

Listen to some of the best moments from HayHouseRadio.com, featuring expert authors such as Dr. Christiane Northrup, Anthony William, Caroline Myss, James Van Praagh, and Doreen Virtue discussing topics such as health, self-healing, motivation, spirituality, positive psychology, and personal development.

Hay House Live Podcast

Enjoy a selection of insightful and inspiring lectures from Hay House Live, an exciting event series that features Hay House authors and leading experts in the fields of alternative health, nutrition, intuitive medicine, success, and more! Feel the electricity of our authors engaging with a live audience, and get motivated to live your best life possible!

Find Hay House podcasts on iTunes, or visit
www.HayHouse.com/podcasts for more info.

HAY HOUSE

Look within

Join the conversation about latest products,
events, exclusive offers and more.

f Hay House UK

🐦 @HayHouseUK

📷 @hayhouseuk

♥ healyourlife.com

We'd love to hear from you!